W9-AEB-335

Whoever Tells the Best Story Wins

Whoever Tells the Best Story Wins

*How to Use
Your Own Stories
to Communicate with
Power and Impact*

Annette Simmons

AMACOM

American Management Association

New York • Atlanta • Brussels • Chicago
Mexico City • San Francisco • Shanghai
Tokyo • Toronto • Washington, D.C.

Special discounts on bulk quantities of AMACOM books are
available to corporations, professional associations, and other
organizations. For details, contact Special Sales Department,
AMACOM, a division of American Management Association,
1601 Broadway, New York, NY 10019.
Tel: 212-903-8316. Fax: 212-903-8083.
E-mail: specialsls@amanet.org
Website: www.amacombooks.org/go/specialsales
To view all AMACOM titles go to: www.amacombooks.org

This publication is designed to provide accurate and authoritative
information in regard to the subject matter covered. It is sold with the
understanding that the publisher is not engaged in rendering legal,
accounting, or other professional service. If legal advice or other expert
assistance is required, the services of a competent professional person
should be sought.

Library of Congress Cataloging-in-Publication Data

Simmons, Annette.
    Whoever tells the best story wins : how to use your own stories to communicate
with power and impact / Annette Simmons.
      p. cm.
    Includes bibliographical references and index.
    ISBN-13: 978-0-8144-0914-5
    ISBN-10: 0-8144-0914-8
    1. Business communication.   2. Storytelling.   I. Title.

HF5718.S562 2007
658.4'52—dc22   2006036889

© 2007 Annette Simmons.
All rights reserved.
Printed in the United States of America.

This publication may not be reproduced,
stored in a retrieval system,
or transmitted in whole or in part,
in any form or by any means, electronic,
mechanical, photocopying, recording, or otherwise,
without the prior written permission of AMACOM,
a division of American Management Association,
1601 Broadway, New York, NY 10019.

Printing number

10 9 8 7 6 5 4 3 2 1

Dedicated to Ray Hicks
August 29, 1922–April 21, 2003

Thank you for your stories.

Contents

Acknowledgments

My father raised me to be a storyteller. When I was a tyke, he engaged me with his original fable about a lion and a marmoset monkey. He encouraged my self-confidence with stories of his early business exploits (catching minnows), warned me against rash judgments by describing the dissolution of that enterprise (one minnow for you, one for me, one for you, one for me. . . .). And for all the other stories you told me, thank you Dad.

My mother raised me to be creative. I was never allowed to say "I'm bored." If there was a newspaper nearby it was all I needed to make a pirate hat, papier-maché elephant, or cheerleader pompoms, to name three of a thousand options. She took me to watercolor and oil painting classes, arranged piano lessons and even saved my flute from junior high up until a few years ago, just in case. Because of you I am never bored, thank you Mom.

To my loyal friends Sherry and Brandy Decker, thank you for letting me be your sister. To Casey and Shelby Lake thanks for letting me be your Auntie Net.

To Pam McGrath and Doug Lipman, how could I have survived without you?

To Meena Wilson, I cherish your friendship and am thrilled to see your success.

To Beth and Jennifer, thank you for watching over Larry and

Lucy. I sleep better on the road knowing how well you care for them.

To Perry Mandanis, your generosity, creativity, deep understanding, and friendship have been invaluable. Thank you for being my friend.

*I find that most people know what a
story is until they sit down to write one.*
—FLANNERY O'CONNOR

Whoever Tells the Best Story Wins

Introduction

MY MATERNAL GRANDFATHER was a top salesman for Kellogg's in the 1940s and 1950s. He was funny, outgoing, and he loved practical jokes. In my favorite photo, he sits ramrod straight with the face of a general on a pony so short his toes graze the ground. I never met him but his stories were part of my growing up. Story jokes were popular back in his day. Here is an old one but a good one that helps illustrate the role stories play in communication.

A man walks into a pet store and says, "I want a talking parrot."

The clerk says, "Yes sir, I have several birds that talk. This large green parrot here is quite a talker." He taps on the cage, and the bird says, "The Lord is my Shepherd, I shall not want." He knows the entire Bible by heart. "This red one here is young but he's learning." He prompted, "Polly want a cracker." And the bird repeated back, "Polly want a cracker." Then I've got a mynah bird but he belonged to a sailor, so if you have children you won't want that one."

The man says, "I'll take the younger one, if you can teach me how to make him talk."

"Sure I can teach you," said the pet store owner. He

sat down with the man and spent hours teaching him how to train the parrot. Then he put the bird in the cage, took his money, and sent the man home to start his training regimen.

After a week the man came back into the store very irritated. "That bird you sold me doesn't talk."

"He doesn't? Did you follow my instructions?" asked the clerk.

"Yep, to the letter," replied the man.

"Well, maybe that bird is lonely. I tell you what. I'll sell you this little mirror here and you put it in the cage. That bird will see his reflection and he will start talking right away," responded the clerk.

The man did as he was told but three days later was back in the shop. "I'm thinking of asking for my money back, that bird won't talk."

The shop owner pondered a bit and said, "I bet that bird is bored. He needs some toys. Here, take this bell—no charge. Put it in the bird's cage. I bet he'll start talking once he has something to do."

In a week the man was back angrier than ever. He walked in carrying a shoebox, "That bird you sold me died." He opened the shoebox and there was his poor little dead parrot. "I want my money back."

The shop owner was horrified, "I'm so sorry, I don't know what happened. But . . . tell me . . . did the bird ever even *try* to talk?"

"Well," said the man, "he did say one word, right before he fell off his perch and died."

"What did he say?" the clerk inquired.

The man replied, "Fo-o-o-o-od."

Poor parrot, he was starving to death. That parrot needed food the way we need stories. Most communications designed to influence are as stimulating to us as a mirror and bell are to a starving parrot. What little substance there is, is like candy—empty calories devoid of nutrition that feeds core human needs. People need more from you. They want to feel your presence in your message, to taste a trace of humanity that proves there is a "you" (individually or collectively) sending them this message. The absence of human presence in today's high-tech lifestyle leaves people starved for attention. Stories help people feel acknowledged, connected, and less alone. Your stories help them feel more alive by proving there is another live person out there somewhere sending them that message.

This joke does that for you and me: it tells you about me as a person. For instance, you now know my family has a sick sense of humor. You've met my grandfather and know that I loved him very much. As a bonus, the joke also illustrates a powerful way to examine your approach to communication. Do you concentrate on "bells and mirrors" like measurable frequencies, reach, and clarity in a way that might cause you to forget the food of human connection that fuels the desire to receive communication in the first place? Communication is never an end goal. Communication is always a *means* to a goal that ultimately can be boiled down to one simple objective: meeting human needs—yours, theirs, and ours. Once food and shelter needs are met, the rest of our needs are psychological. Our psychological needs are met or unmet based on the stories we tell ourselves and each other about what matters most and who controls it.

A perfectly happy customer can suddenly feel unhappy after hearing a story that another customer got a better product at half the price, then be satisfied again when you assure him that this story was not true and circulated by a competitor who didn't have all the facts. Nothing physically changed, but the stories about reality completely change perceptions of what is true, important, and thus, real.

Stories interpret raw facts and proofs to create reality. Change the story and you change the meaning of the facts. "Man stabs son" could be interpreted as a murder or a life-saving emergency tracheotomy, depending on the story that you tell. To understand the power stories wield is both an incredible opportunity and awesome responsibility. The stories that best deliver the food of human connection are more likely to construct mental realities that have physical consequences. A real estate developer who produces a picture book of the history of the land from school children's drawings has a better chance of getting a permit than a developer with a PowerPoint presentation on economic development.

It is not necessarily the physical properties of a yacht, fancy car, white teeth, or thin body that people want. What they truly want are the feelings and sensations that those things might bring them. People crave confirmation of a self-image that makes them feel important, desirable, and good. Ultimately all humans want the attention of other human beings in a way that makes us feel important, desirable, powerful, and alive. Services and goods are satisfying only if they deliver the food of human connection. The stories you tell, and the stories people tell themselves about you and your product or service, enhance or minimize your ability to deliver satisfaction.

The sense of human presence in communication is frequently elbowed out by "criteria" designed to make communication clear, bite-sized, and attention grabbing, but which instead oversimplifies, truncates, and irritates. These "subgoals" often obscure the real goal: human connection. Communication can't feel genuine without the distinctive personality of a human being to provide context. You need to show up when you communicate: the real you, not the polished idealized you.

The missing ingredient in most failed communication is humanity. This is an easy fix. In order to blend humanity into every communication you send all you have to do is tell more stories and bingo—you just showed up. Your communication now has a human presence. Use this book to integrate more stories into your communication, and I guarantee you will develop presence. More importantly, you will reconnect to bigger stories that frame your life and your work in a way that fills your life with meaning and guides others to seek the same.

People float in an ocean of data and disconnected facts that overwhelm them with choices. According to Barry Schwartz, author of *The Paradox of Choice: Why More is Less* (Ecco, 2004), "There's a point where all of this choice starts to be not only unproductive, but counterproductive—a source of pain, regret, worry about missed opportunities and unrealistically high expectations."

In this ocean of choice, a meaningful story can feel like a life preserver that tethers us to something safe, important, or at the very least more solid than disembodied voices begging for attention.

PART ONE

Thinking in Story

CHAPTER 1

Story Thinking
What Does That Even Mean?

ONCE UPON A TIME, before you learned to be more objective, you thought you were important and that the people around you were important. Chances are you asked questions that made other people uncomfortable. To protect you from a life of narcissistic, emotional waywardness, you were sent to school to learn how to be useful. You learned the scientific method. You learned you aren't important. You are actually just a dot on a bell curve. If you are lucky, your dot was two standard deviations from the mean and you were deemed "gifted," which is objectively very similar to being "important." Later you learned that nothing is true if you can't test it and can't prove it is true in repeated experiments. Critical thinking, rational analysis, and objective thinking prepared you to put emotions aside and make better decisions.

Since then, making objective, unemotional decisions has served you well. You can prove things are true with cost/benefit analyses, models, and bar charts so other people can see when you are "right" and know your recommendations are "right." However, being right has lost its luster. Like any good scientist, you have gathered data that *proves* being right doesn't mean people listen to you. You may even have begun to suspect that everyone you work with is two standard deviations from the mean and not in the "gifted" direction. In fact, there seems to be no significant correlation between being right and creating compliance.

Like most of us educated in the twentieth century, you've come to the conclusion that clear communications, objective thinking, and rational decision making has its limitations when applied to the unclear, subjective, and multirational (everyone has their own ratio these days) world. If you are ready to acknowledge the limitations of objective thinking you are also ready to entertain the idea that subjective thinking is not as irrelevant as you were taught. As a scientist you can observe that people insist upon behaving as if they are important and the people around them are important. They may say they think in objective, rational ways, but every important decision they make is based on interpreting objective data in terms of how it affects them and those they love. Decisions are always subjective.

Here's a Thought. . . .

What if we develop a tool that is specifically dedicated to diagnose, analyze, and intervene on those subjective interpretations? What could you do with such a tool? You could identify the bizarre interpretations that another culture or another person might place on your clear, rational communications. You could predict the subjective spin people might give to your objectively derived decisions. You could even influence them to see things the way you see them. What would you pay for such a tool? $19.95? But wait, there's more.

This tool not only helps you influence others, it also helps you self-govern. Have you found lately that you know what you *should* do, but try as hard as you might, you just didn't *feel* like it. Perhaps you were in a situation where you *knew* you should be patient, compassionate, or perhaps more firm, but time and energy were in short supply and you just didn't have it in you. This tool will pop your view of the situation so you can instantaneously remember who you are and why you are here in a way that reframes time and renews your energy. Lots of wonderful things can happen in the subjective world. You are no longer bound by linear, rational frameworks. Magic can happen. Miracles surprise you, and people become important again, even you.

When you stimulate human emotions with a story, you point those emotions in a certain direction. At a social level, stories replicate the neurological effect of attention in our individual brains. Society attends to what draws our attention, and what draws society's attention is tended. People don't consciously decide to forget a politician's sexual peccadillo; it is just that the threat of war grabs our attention.

Experiment by directing your attention to a past event to see if you can create emotions or even behaviors. Remember your first puppy love. Spend some time remembering how old you were, the hairstyles and clothing of that time. Remember the awkward silences or worse, the babbling nonsense. In your mind's eye lie on your childhood bed once again and think about how much attention you gave every interaction, potential interaction, and fantasized interaction with your heart's desire. Stay there until you feel a ghost of the feelings you felt then. Do you feel a slight urge to action? Perhaps you want to find out "where is that person now?"

Now steal yourself for a less pleasant trip. Let's go to high school and pull up a memory of an embarrassing rejection. Any public humiliation will do, just choose one. If you are like most people, high school was full of them. Give that embarrassing memory all of your attention. Remember names, see the place, reenact the scene. Now notice the ghosts of the feelings you felt then as they reignite. You may feel a tug toward actions that prevent this kind of experience.

This experiment demonstrates how attention—attending to a memory—alters your present reality by changing your feelings and erecting filters that interpret the present. In the same way stories become society's memories that pull the attention of large

groups of people to certain feelings and frames that filter perceptions of current events. An article about a current politician can
reference Nixon or Lincoln in a way that shadows or brightens
readers' interpretation of the facts presented.

Likewise when you tell a story that both draws attention and
is often retold within a group, you in effect control future feelings
and filters about that subject. If you control the feelings and filters
of enough people you can alter their conclusions about reality.
Attention is a prerequisite to influence because attention frames
interpretations. When a movie director makes a little box with
his hands to emphasize what is seen in the frame, he also deletes
most of the surrounding data. Similarly, when you frame an issue
you predetermine the conclusions people draw from available data
by focusing their attention on the data inside your frame.

In George Lakoff's *Don't Think of an Elephant,* the renowned
linguist does an excellent job of describing how framing an issue
dramatically influences perceptions. When you control attention
you control conclusions. His entire book makes the point that
whoever tells the best story wins. The most cohesive and powerful
story pulls people's attention so powerfully that very few think to
override that pull. Once you give your attention to the title *Don't
Think of an Elephant,* no matter how hard you try you cannot *not*
think of an elephant. It is the same way with stories.

The really important issues of this world are ultimately decided by the story that grabs the most attention and is repeated
most often. Although objective criteria cannot guarantee a subjective outcome, objective criteria are still important.

Subjective Is NOT the Opposite of Objective

Objective thinking is important, valuable, and unimpaired by
subjective thinking. Learning to use a subjective thinking tool will
not erode your ability to think in objective terms. You will still be

able to conduct a cost/benefit ratio or analysis with the best of them. By adding subjective thinking to your repertoire you add another tool that increases your ability to assemble the many different interpretations that might be drawn from your objective data. Knowing these ahead of time helps you predict, understand, and influence interpretations before they are set in stone. You already know how to use numbers—the language of objective thinking—to great benefit. What you may not realize is that you also know more about the language of the subjective that you suspect.

The language of the subjective is *story*. Story is how humans interpret things as good or bad, important or irrelevant, safe or dangerous, and who is "one of us" or "one of them." These subjective interpretations do not degrade objective thinking but enhance objective thinking so that you can forecast how your obviously "rational" decisions will be embraced by irrational humans.

Look at this diagram:

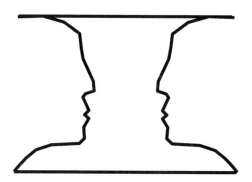

What do you see? Exactly. Either two faces, or a candlestick/ chalice/cake plate. This diagram demonstrates how using both objective and subjective thinking works. You can see two completely different pictures from the same input. The tough part is that you can't see both at the same time. Go ahead and try, I'll wait. See? You can switch back and forth really, really fast—but the brain can't let it be two things at once. Similarly, your brain likes the objective tools you've been using to identify what is "true" and "false." Adding subjective tools is difficult for those who are particularly good at rational objective thinking, and vice versa. Some gifted individuals do both as naturally as a child prodigy plays the piano. However, most of us lean to one side or the other. My hope is that this book will help objective thinkers embrace the subjective, and help subjective thinkers better communicate with the objective thinkers.

Story as Subjective Thinking Tool

Because human behavior is so subjective, objective thinking can actually distort your ability to analyze, understand, or predict human behavior. You may have been taught that subjective information is irrelevant . . . well, *not to the subject*. Humans experience this world from eyes and ears set in a body that can only be in one place at a time. The collective past, present, and imagined future times and places represent a subjective point of view that frames how a person feels about you, your idea, or your organization.

Storytelling transports people to different points of view so they can reinterpret or reframe what your "facts" mean to them. Consider the idea of rational thinking. The term rational comes from "ratio," which is a basic assumption in decision making: the ratio of cost to benefit. Yet ratios are based on subjective criteria. For instance, papayas are useless to a person who dislikes them whereas they are simultaneously valuable to the person who enjoys them—even if the cost/benefit ratio for each papaya is the same. When a papaya-hater trades one papaya for two oranges with a papaya-lover, their combined cost/benefit ratios create a mutual experience of an "equal exchange," even if not a mathematically equal exchange.

It sounds easier than it is to suspend objective thinking for subjective thinking. When high achievers (hello) employ subjective reasoning, the paradox, ambiguities, and contradictions can drive your internal critic crazy over the unscientific and anecdotal nature of stories. Your internal critic usually seeks to discredit and discount mutually exclusive or irrational interpretations of the facts, in order to find the one that is "right." But the ability to see and deeply understand multiple interpretations is what makes you smarter. Stories are anecdotes—unscientific in statistical terms. In terms of human history, science is a recent adaptation. Stories communicate in the way humans used to think and communicate before we discovered science. Actually stories represent the way human brains *still* think regardless of our rational pretense. Rational thinking is a tool of analysis that stops at the frontal lobes.

Stories communicate directly with the old brain, the limbic system, the amygdala, and the other core parts of the brain that only acknowledge tangible reality, not symbols of reality, like numbers and language. The "feeling" parts of the brain are designed to fast-track responses (approach/avoid/freeze) to important experiences (good/bad), based on smell, sight, touch, taste, and feel. Stories ignite imagined sensory experiences that represent reality way better than numbers plotted along a bar chart.

Here is a story that conveys an experience of the sort of perceptual agility storytelling delivers:

> An old farmer patiently spent part of each afternoon talking with a nosy neighbor, who visited him about the same time every day.
>
> One afternoon during his daily visit, the neighbor suddenly exclaimed, "Did you buy a new horse? Yesterday you only had one horse, now I see two."
>
> The farmer told the neighbor how this horse, unmarked and apparently without an owner, wandered into his barn. He explained that he had asked everyone

he knew, and since no one owned the horse he decided he would care for it until they found its owner.

The neighbor said, "You are such a lucky man. Yesterday you had only one horse and today you have two." The farmer said, "Perhaps, we shall see."

The next day the farmer's son tried to ride the new horse. He fell and broke his leg. That afternoon the neighbor said, "You are an unlucky man. Your son now can't help you in the fields." The farmer said, "Perhaps, we shall see."

The third day the army came through the village looking for young men to conscript to fight. The farmer's son was not taken because he had a broken leg. The neighbor again said, "You are a lucky man," and again the farmer said, "Perhaps, we shall see."

Subjective point of view changes meaning. Meaning is more powerful than facts. If people fear the meaning of your facts they can easily distort, discredit, or ignore them. Likewise, if they like the meaning (subjectively) of your facts, they embrace, use, and even embellish your facts. Actions result from the stories people tell themselves about what objective facts mean to them.

Look back at the diagram again to simulate how it feels to toggle back and forth between the subjective and objective points of view. Think about how often we argue about what is and isn't true. Notice how two mutually exclusive things can be true, depending on how you look at it. We can avoid most of our time wasting arguments once we realize that two interpretations (or seven, or ninety-five interpretations) are "right" depending on the point of view. By using this tool wisely we can reclaim wasted time that is better spent factoring the impact of different interpretations into our decision making, implementation plans, and marketing campaigns.

The ability to see multiple points of view may feel like a liability in an adversarial situation. It is sometimes perceived as a lack of clarity, a lack of direction, even as a lack of discipline. Subjective reasoning has a time and a place and must be approached judiciously and with wisdom. You or your listeners may feel some anxiety when you intentionally invoke story as a direct feed to the limbic system. People have spent time and energy learning how to exclude emotions from decision making. Many won't welcome the emotions back with open arms. However, storytelling doesn't bring emotions *back* to decision making. Storytelling gives us *access* to the emotions that will occur as a result of your decision whether you acknowledge them or not.

So yes, subjective reasoning can feel dangerous to people who were trained to believe emotions degrade decision making. As a psychiatrist friend of mine put it, a blind man who could suddenly see would not poke his eyes out just because some of the things he saw were horrible. Likewise, subjective thinking is simply a new channel of interpretation that will bring both good and bad news. Regardless, it brings you vital information you need if you want to influence others.

If you are the only person in the room using story as a tool, understand why and how people will resist this new tool. Be sensitive to people's sincere desire to make good decisions. They've been trained for decades that emotions and anecdotal evidence is "bad." This book is designed to help you lay the groundwork for using story as a credible tool. Understand that allowing the emotions back into decision making can be very destabilizing for people whose entire lives are designed to be objective and rational. Storytelling in a work situation can awaken long denied emotions about personal decisions in a way that surprises and can frighten people who convinced themselves emotions don't matter. Be gentle. Story is a very powerful tool. When you activate new stories you transport people to new points of view, change meaning, behavior, and in that way—you change the future.

CHAPTER 2

What Is Story?

WE NEED A clear definition of story that translates immediately to useful application. But first I want to unravel
some of the misconceptions you may have about storytelling and your talents as a storyteller. Too many people think
"I'm not a good storyteller." Horsefeathers. If you are breathing
you are a storyteller. Moreover, you have talent.

Simply taking the time to read this book means you have the
one natural talent necessary to become a wonderful storyteller—
the talent of curiosity. You were curious enough to get this book
so you are way ahead of the game. Your curiosity causes you to
pay attention to what others think and feel is important, to the
human details; you listen to other people's stories. Listening is
observable evidence of curiosity. Over-confidence, the opposite of
curiosity (also known as arrogance) makes a storyteller preachy,
boring, and disrespectful.

Know-it-alls don't make good storytellers. These are the people who buy books that promise to teach how to "influence anyone to do anything." They actually think they deserve that kind
of influence. I can't teach you that. Actually, no one can teach
even them how to "influence anyone to do anything" because it isn't
possible. It is a myth. It is a big fat lie. No one on earth has that

much influence and no one deserves that much influence. Those who believe the myth are in danger of following false prophets.

One story that exposes the myth of absolute influence is the story of King Midas. Remember? King Midas wished that everything he touched would turn to gold and he got what he wished for. The food he touched turned to gold. He couldn't eat. He picked up an apple and before he could bite into it, it turned to gold. Much worse, his daughter ran up to him and the second he reached down to pick her up his touch turned her into a statue of gold. He killed his own daughter. You see, 100 percent influence is 100 percent isolation. You don't want it.

In some cases "no" is the best thing that could happen to you. I don't know about you, but there have been times when I was truly grateful no one listened to me. I was so sure I was right, too. But if they had listened to me it would've been a disaster.

When you get a "no," you are on the trail of a new story. It means that person knows or believes they know something you don't yet understand. Either way you need to find out. "No" can be a gift. It's your opportunity to hear *their* story. Storytellers approach influence as a reciprocal process that flows both ways. To be a good storyteller you must be a good story listener. I've never met a good storyteller who wasn't equally good at listening to stories. Where do you think they find their stories?

Experience Reconstituted

But what is a story? There are a thousand definitions, mostly academic, quite accurate but not very instructional. For our purposes our working definition of story is:

Story is a reimagined experience narrated with enough detail and feeling to cause your listeners' imaginations to experience it as real.

Experience is the best teacher . . . always has been, always will be. If we could magically transport the people we wish to influence into a life-changing experience we could change the world. Imagine popping a certain software engineer into your client's daily life so he could personally experience the frustration of bugs in the system. Or better, let's place a deserving politician into the body of a low-income, single mother's life for just one day. It's a sweet fantasy to imagine a guy who doesn't even pick up his own dry cleaning shopping in a supermarket with three unruly children, trying to buy fresh fruits and vegetables on minimum wage. That politician would never forget that experience.

Direct experience is the Scrooge method of education. Transport your short-sighted boss, coworker, customer, or teenager to a place and time that leaves an indelible experience in the deepest parts of their brain. Way below the intellectual knowing, personal experience delivers deep understanding that allows true empathy and challenges false clarity of entrenched positions or slick politics. Put an investor to work in a sweat shop in an underdeveloped country and then ask if it is possible to better monitor suppliers' working conditions. If we could GIVE them the experience, it would change their minds, alter their decisions, and create cohesive action in the right directions.

Yet, the best tool to influence others—experience—isn't feasible in most cases. Kidnapping, even for good reason, is frowned upon. The best we can do is to bring the experience to them through a story that is so vivid it feels as if they are actually there.

Let's say you want to create trust with new employees, or more likely with old ones disgruntled by the last reorganization. The best way to build trust is for them, over time, to experience you keeping your agreements, acting with integrity, and holding confidences secure. Over time, the entire group personally experiences you as trustworthy, and they decide to trust your decisions and to trust you without second-guessing, arguments, or passive resistance.

The problem of course is that you don't have time to build up that track record. You need cooperation now. Worse, in real life people rarely experience your keeping your agreements or acting with integrity because they aren't there when it happens, or when you tried to keep your agreements you were over-ruled. They can never know what it costs you to go to bat for them—at least not firsthand. Other people can only experience an incomplete and imperfect sample of who you are. They only see little glimpses— usually out of context—which quite frankly don't showcase your better side.

Think about a typical day. You wake up with great (okay, good) expectations of having a productive day. Then the kids spill their cereal and the dog jumps on your freshly cleaned trousers. Some idiot cuts you off in traffic. And your day is up and down, like most days. You get to work, and the up and down continues. The phone rings with news that you got the big client you wanted. You decide to tell the team at a staff meeting that afternoon, maybe buy some doughnuts. Three hours later, after slaving over exhaustive and questionably relevant reports due yesterday, you see two staff members putting golf balls instead of working. Suddenly a new policy about playing golf in the hallway becomes your first order of business at the staff meeting and your enthusiasm about winning the new business has waned by the time you get around to announcing it.

My question to you is: *When* during this typical up-and-down day does your team experience you? When you are happy, productive, and at your best? Or when you are disappointed and frustrated? Most of us have to admit we are not that noticeable when we are happy and productive. We sort of fade into the woodwork. The times we seek attention are the times when we think a correction needs to be made. Indeed we are almost addicted to correction. Monitor and correct. Monitor and correct. The problem with that is that people's experiences of you become skewed to the negative.

the kind of results you'd like to see at work, in your family, and in your community. When you turn your attention to these stories you can be more intentional in creating the kind of perceptions that achieve goals rather than reinforce problems. These are the six types of stories I recommend you invest with your time and attention:

Who-I-Am Stories

What qualities earn you the right to influence this person? Tell of a time, place, or event that provides evidence that you have these qualities. Reveal who you are as a person. Do you have kids? What were you like as a kid? What did your parents teach you? What did you learn in your first job? Get personal. People need to know who you are before they can trust you.

Why-I-Am-Here Stories

When someone assumes you are there to sell an idea that will cost them money, time, or resources, it immediately discredits your "facts" as biased. However, you chose your job for reasons besides money. Tell this person what you get out of it besides money. Or if it is just about the money for you, own it.

Teaching Stories

Certain lessons are best learned from experience—some of them over and over again during a lifetime. Patience, for instance. You can tell someone to "be patient," but it's rarely helpful. Better to tell a story that creates a shared experience (simulated, of course) of patience along with the rewards of patience. Your story will change behavior much better than advice. Story is as close to modeling patience as you can get in three minutes.

Vision Stories

A worthy, exciting future story reframes present difficulties as "worth it." Big projects and new challenges are difficult and frustrating for implementers who weren't in on the decision. Without a vision, these meaningless frustrations suck the life energy out of a group. With an engaging vision, however, huge obstacles shrink to small irritants on the path to a worthwhile goal. (*Note*: Vision stories that promise more than they deliver do more damage than good.)

Values-in-Action Stories

Values are subjective. To one person, integrity means doing what his boss tells him to do. To someone else, integrity means saying no even if it costs her job. If you want to encourage a value or teach a value you have to provide a "demonstration" by telling a story that illustrates in action what that value means, behaviorally. Hypothetical situations sound hypocritical and preachy. Be specific.

I-Know-What-You-Are-Thinking Stories

People like to stay safe. Many times they have already made up their mind, with specific objections to the ideas you bring. They don't come out and say, "I've already decided this is hogwash," but they might be thinking it. It is a trust-building surprise for you to share their secret suspicions in a story that first validates and then dispels these objections without sounding defensive.

* * * * *

Before we move on to developing and testing stories we need to return to the issue of subjective and objective thinking. I hope I've done a good job demonstrating that stories are subjective, and that subjective doesn't mean irrelevant. Now let's address the specific ways that subjective story thinking breaks three rules you learned when you were taught to think objectively. It is much easier to develop your storytelling skills when you suspend your internal critic's message that you are breaking important rules for good thinking. We have to create a new category of good thinking that may be substantially different but is just as valid as objective thinking.

CHAPTER 3

Training Your Brain

GOOD STORYTELLING IS not a skill set. It is not achieved by following a recipe. Skill sets and recipes only work on mechanical things and systems that don't think for themselves. Things that *do* think for themselves—humans—have no reliable operator manual or blueprint. Thus we can never have a reliable recipe or skill set for storytelling. At best we can learn to adopt a frame of reference that reveals the stories and subjective interpretations at play.

Storytelling flows from a particular state of mind. Good storytellers live in, or can step into, a philosophical framework that is different from how most of us usually think. Once you have a map of this philosophical frame you can step into it at will. My guess is that you won't want to live there because it's not the best philosophical framework for making tons of money—ask any professional storyteller. However, it is a philosophical framework of big truths, moving stories, and deep connections. Things that bullet points fail to achieve. Stories bring hope, faith, perseverance, and other good yet irrational emotions back into our daily lives.

You can train your brain to "think in story." But first you must unplug your brain from thinking in charts, metrics, and spreadsheets. These kinds of summarizing devices are the culprits that block your imagination from thinking in story. Stories are undigested, presummary, preconclusion reports of actual experiences. Imagination is engaged because the experience is still ambiguous in the way real life is ambiguous. Stories don't squeeze out interpretation—they invite listeners to participate in the "what does this mean?" question. Stories give people freedom to come to their own conclusions. People who reject predigested conclusions might just agree with your interpretations if you get out of their face long enough for them to see what you have seen.

You may desperately want people to come to the "right" conclusions, but trying to control their conclusions pushes people away. Story is more trusting and thus more trustworthy. Trust and trustworthiness are inseparable in real life. Trust operates along patterns of reciprocity based on assumptions about intent that linear analysis can't accurately represent. Reciprocity is one of the most reliable predictors of human behavior. In fact, the field of economics has developed an entire field—experimental economics—to understand how perceptions operate on economic decisions. Economic decisions in real life are often not rational. Our emotions cause us to punish those we perceive as free-riders even when it costs us and take irrational risks (no guarantee of return) to encourage reciprocal returns from strangers. This economically irrational risk is called trusting someone. Trust is one of the first things to disappear when all decisions are forced to make objective, rational sense.

Temporarily abandoning well-rewarded skills could leave you feeling untethered. For some it feels downright irresponsible. However, the skills that make you a winner in competition are skills that protect, define, segment, clarify, and "own." These thinking skills protect you from mediocrity by defining goals, drawing lines of distinction, clarifying roles, comparing measures of quality, and pursuing zero defects. Yet, they forge a philosophical framework that compares and divides. The framework of story connects and inspires. We need both.

Metrics, analysis, and objective thinking are tools that protect you from repeating mistakes by breaking things down into manageable pieces or revealing root causes. Root cause, disassembly, and reassembly work on any systems made up of machines that don't think or made up of people who reliably will let you do their thinking for them. The military used to be that way, but even the military faces an explosive diversity of thinking and obedience based on agreement. Cultural differences, past experiences, and the Internet fuels independent thinking into wildly diverse opinions on what is right and how to go about it.

Very smart people have tried to design measurements and thinking tools to measure and thus control subjective issues like trust, loyalty, faith, respect, engagement, and inspiration. However, none of these feeling states is reliably measurable. You can measure behaviors that in *some* situations represent one subjective definition of trust. However, real trust-in-action is too situational for one definition to be meaningful for an entire company, government, or community. For instance, there are times when trust means you keep your mouth shut and protect a coworker. There are times when trust means you protect your coworker from making the same mistake twice by speaking up. It depends on the situation. Applying measurements to subjective dynamics like trust only distorts, or worse, discredits what we "know in our hearts." Like quantum physics, the very act of measuring it, alters it. We have to get past the mantra "if you can't measure it, you can't manage it."

The natural way to describe and "manage" subjective issues is to pay attention to the stories we tell. Once we do that we can stop trying to measure what can't be measured and spend more time managing that which we can't measure. Unless you are a social scientist, continuing to spend resources in an effort to measure trust leads you further away from the real thing. Worse, it might trick you into a false confidence that meeting your numbers has achieved "trustworthiness." Hypocrisy thrives when metrics are valued more than personal experience. And because there seems to be an extended time lag between lost trust and bad numbers, once the numbers decline it is too late.

The danger in the adage "if you can't measure it, you can't manage it" is that people believe it is true. If you can't measure it you sure as hell better be managing it, every day, with attention, integrity, and self-examination. Accountability needs to stretch beyond that which can be counted. Einstein is popularly thought to have said, "Not everything that can be counted counts, and not everything that counts can be counted." The sheer volume of well-intended measurements we are forced to gather, analyze, and attend disconnects us from our own good judgment and sense of personal responsibility for creating situational and subjective solutions. Storytelling reestablishes accountability for human qualities that numbers distort or miss completely.

Story protects us from apathy, mistrust, disrespect, disconnection, and disillusionment by reconnecting us to commitment, trust, respect, and inspiration. Developing your ability to use storytelling to increase accountability will not erase your talents in objective, rational thinking. You can still be objective and rational when you are done. The additional skill is that you can also be subjective and "multirational" as well. The trick is to develop enough agility to toggle back and forth between objective and subjective frameworks at will.

No *Proof*

The hardest habit to suspend is our litmus test of expecting proof before you acknowledge anything as "true." You probably were trained to demand proof, to seek excellence (zero defects), and to apply linear analysis to compare and contrast alternatives. These thinking tools keep you from being duped, tricked, or otherwise misled so you don't drop a good defense without good reason. The reason to temporarily liberate input from the burden of proof is that there are no reliable proofs for feelings. Think about it: If your spouse says, "If you love me, prove it," what do you do? Buy your spouse a car? Tell your mother to butt out? Or stop buying flowers and start washing the dishes? My point is that love cannot be proved by objective standards. Too many times, important information has been disregarded because, without proof, it was dismissed.

Proof does not exist in the subjective frame. In the subjective frame, nothing is true more than 50 to 70 percent of the time. (I made these numbers up, okay? Think of them as a metaphor.) Consider a happily married couple. Ask one spouse, "Do you love your wife?" And his answer may be "yes" on Friday night after a romantic dinner. Ask the same man on Saturday morning when he is late for tee time and his car is on "empty" because she used all his gas and didn't refill it. If he is honest, he will have to report that what he feels toward his wife in that moment is something other than love. The answer to any questions about feelings, values, or attitudes (all subjective) is "it depends."

Another example. I like to think I'm smart. I've written several books, been hired to help important people think through important decisions, and yet when I was in Hawaii and saw a glorious sunset, I got up very early the next morning and went to the same spot waiting to see an equally glorious sunrise. It wasn't until the sun hit my back that I reluctantly realized that while the sun goes down in the west it tends to come up in the east. I can "prove" that I am both smart *and* unbelievably stupid depending on the situation. This is an example of how nothing is reliably true or false because human beings are paradoxes of good and bad, smart and stupid, generous and greedy, etc.

If you embrace (temporarily) that nothing is "true" about

human feelings more than 50 to 70 percent of the time, it means you have to lower your standards (keep breathing) in seeking and refining stories to tell. You can't find perfection and you distort things when you try. The only way to approach storytelling is to embrace the ambiguity and imperfections of human experience.

Forget zero defects when dealing with subjective issues. The 50-to-70-percent success rate applies to tools that help you find stories, the strategies of telling good stories, as well as the impact your stories will have on others. These tools work at best 70 percent of the time. Good technique (for example, "confident" tone) might improve your story in one situation yet alienate listeners in another situation. No one story will reach 100 percent of your target with the exact outcome you desire. A good rule of thumb for those of us who don't know when to stop chasing perfection is that one story will only be meaningful to about 70 percent of the people you hope to influence. That level of reliability means you must diversify your portfolio and spread your risk by telling more stories. It also means you have to increase your tolerance for failure. Think in terms of million-dollar baseball players: a batting average of 300 still means that they strike out twice as often as they hit the ball. Once you expect to miss the mark some of the time you don't ditch storytelling just because one story fails. You tell another story, or better, ask someone to tell you a story.

So can we improve the tool of storytelling to create better reliability? Not unless you can redesign the human body and brain. The complexity is unavoidable. If you want senior management to delay a decision, don't just tell them one story, tell them three stories. Expect that you will always leave one or two people unmoved. Once you define acceptable losses, it is clear that telling three stories is more time effective and more authentic than trying to force one story to work for everyone. The trick is to temporarily silence the critical voice that rejects a detail, description, or event after a single trial. It takes a wide net to scoop up the human and humane experiences and feelings that are the stuff of good stories.

Stories live in the messy ambiguity of real life. If you clean them up too much you kill them.

Nonlinear Relationships

Now that we've temporarily lowered your standards we must also temporarily redefine cause and effect. Your expectations of cause and effect are probably grounded in the physical sciences. One plus one equals two. The neural network of the brain is not linear. It makes connections that are exponential, lateral, and dynamic between people, events, and interpretations of those events. One person plus one person could equal Enron or Hewlett Packard. Between humans there are no reliable "one plus one equals two" relationships. Emotions are activated by experientially based associations that lead to illogical but nevertheless strong connections. Say the word "Hawaii" to one person and he may make the following associations: honeymoon . . . sex . . . Viagra . . . spam e-mails. Another person might think Hawaii: Maui. . . . Oprah . . . magazine . . . pick up dry cleaning. The brain is nonlinear and exponentially multirational when it comes to associated thoughts and feelings.

Your habit of objective thinking is embedded with certain assumptions derived from mathematics. One hidden assumption that is problematic for storytelling is the expectation of linear correlations. For instance, we tend to expect big results from big efforts and small results from small efforts. That's true in the physical world, but not in the subjective world of perceptions. In the subjective world of perceptions, little details can make big differences. Imagine your staff listening intently for three hours as you patiently explain the new IT system that is about to be implemented. Then imagine as you walk away you see two staff members rolling their eyes and making quack-quack movements with their hands. Which had more impact? Three hours of attention or that one split second? That is an example of nonlinearity—tiny can equal big. Big can also equal tiny. If your child is dying, losing your job because you have run out of vacation time or sick leave is less important than time with your child. Yet the loss of a job for a healthy family can mean disaster. It all depends on the situation and your point of view.

Nonlinear thinking is difficult because we are so well trained in linear relationships. Most decision-making models do not factor for nonlinear truths. However, with practice you can use linear analysis along with nonlinear analysis to make even better decisions. Consider the example of a boss who has four employees and eight hours of overtime to assign. The linear answer might be:

$$8 \text{ hours divided by } 4 \text{ employees} =$$
$$2 \text{ hours of assigned overtime per employee}$$

The nonlinear answer will take into account that John's kid's birthday is this weekend, and that Billy is saving like crazy to buy a motorcycle. So you check with the others and decide together to give Billy all eight hours of overtime. Both answers are perfectly good ways of analyzing a situation yet produce radically different conclusions. The subjective solution is more stable in terms of staff feelings. Many linear solutions create unnecessary unhappiness because a subjective solution was never sought. But that's another book. For our purposes, put on your objective thinking hat for the numbers, bar charts, and spreadsheet, and then take it off and wear your subjective thinking hat for storytelling.

Temporarily embrace the nonlinear aspects of storytelling. A personal exchange or a story told can impact a relationship in ways that are out of proportion to linear expectations. You can walk into a room and say one right thing and earn trust for a decade—or you can say one wrong thing and blow it for a decade.

That's why linear thinkers get blindsided by emotional response. They don't have a system for anticipating "irrational" and emotionally charged responses. They still think being right is enough.

The truth is your facts aren't as powerful as human emotions. Feelings alter facts, at least the impact of facts. A series of negative experiences that create distrust can make perfectly good facts worthless. If people are mad, sad, or fearful, they discredit facts regardless of the credibility of your process. The upside is that when people feel enthusiastic, valued, and inspired they can attribute more credibility than your facts even deserve. Sometimes people get carried away and even embellish facts. Have you ever had to correct someone who was so excited they overstated the case? "We saved $3 million!" when it was in fact $300,000? That's what happens—perceptions amplify or diminish data.

So, being right is only halfway to action. The rest of the way is through perceptions and feelings. The goal is to alternate back and forth between linear thinking when talking about facts, and nonlinear thinking when telling or interpreting a story. Here's what you need to remember: Details have a HUGE impact. The things that seem irrelevant when crunching numbers are quite relevant when you tell a story about what the numbers mean.

One more cherished assumption to discredit and we are done.

Root-Cause Trap

The last assumption you must temporarily suspend when using storytelling as a tool is the hardest habit to resist. More than likely you have had great results solving problems with the tool of root-cause analysis. When inventory skyrockets, errors increase, or productivity slumps, our immediate response is to perform a root-cause analysis. We track data upstream, isolate the beginning of the problem, find the root cause, and fix it. Again, this works with systems of inanimate objects and obedient people.

However, you may have noticed that obedience ain't what it used to be. When a problem is perceptual, subjective, or emotionally charged, root-cause analysis can actually make things worse.

When morale is low, a staff discussion about why it is low, about who or what is the root cause, is often destructive and blame based. This kind of conversation shifts a group to defensive reasoning. Each group or individual focuses on proving how they are not part of the cause, which sabotages your ability to promote a sense of personal responsibility for the issue. Even if you perfectly identify the root cause, feelings can't be disassembled and reassembled based on what you learned.

However, if you resist the impulse to default to root-cause analysis, you might tell a story, or better, ask staff to tell stories about "Why I choose to work here." Granted you won't get 100 percent response, but one of those stories might just be the shot in the arm everyone needed. I definitely believe you are more likely to improve morale with this approach than with another blame-game, root-cause analysis. Morale is not a function of removing problems. Good morale is when a clear sense of personal gain or personal mission shrinks unavoidable problems from mountains to bumps in the road. The unavoidable problems don't go away—all that changes is perspective and staff perceptions. In the subjective world, the solution often has nothing to do with the problem.

Consider addiction. The root cause of alcoholism is drinking too much alcohol. So from a rational perspective, to cure your addiction you just need to stop drinking too much. However, this approach doesn't have a terribly high success rate. Instead, compare the success of Alcoholics Anonymous, which provides a group experience and twelve steps involving a "higher power." Meetings consist almost entirely of stories. People share their stories of success and failure, loss and forgiveness, and "one day at a time." They share their stories about taking the steps or failing to take the steps. The primary substance of these meetings is telling and listening to stories.

Many social issues are better addressed when we stop trying to impose rational root-cause analysis to problems. The decline in education, for instance, might prompt a linear analysis (this is a massive oversimplification) of math scores dropping to 25 percent of previous levels, indicating that math should be emphasized four times as much. High school students are bored enough. Root-cause analysis only blames the parents, the teachers, the system, or the students. And let's just say we could prove it is the parents' fault. What solution might you propose? Mandatory parental training? More likely education will improve when we stop looking backward in blame and start looking forward with new stories that bring people together around a vision.

In summary storytelling is best applied when three habits are temporarily suspended:

1. The habit of valuing objective proof over reported direct experiences

2. The tendency to define 50-to-70-percent reliability as "unreliable"

3. The expectation that solutions always have a direct and logical relationship with the root cause of a problem

These habits are useful for objective reasoning, but they will distort your understanding of subjective perceptions and emotional reasoning. Its kind of like using your inside voice and your outside voice—both are entirely appropriate depending on whether you are inside or outside. Objective thinking keeps you outside a problem and subjective thinking takes you inside the problem. Both types of understanding are of great value when you seek solutions.

CHAPTER 4

Telling Stories That Win

IF THE PERSON who tells the best story wins, then where do you find these winning stories and how do you learn how to tell them? The practical path to telling winning stories is simply a matter of finding stories that:

1. Communicate your message.

2. You enjoy telling.

3. You actually tell in real-life situations.

Understanding that you should be telling stories and actually telling stories can feel like a chasm to cross for some of us. This is the point at which we leave the hypothetical and get real. Your personal storytelling will be all about you, your stories, and your definition of "win."

You may have noticed that this book offers no overt definitions of "winning." Winning could mean that your efforts ensure that a building project proceeds or that it is cancelled. Winning might mean that your company doubles growth or that your company intentionally forfeits profit to achieve human rights goals. Your definition of "win" is up to you. Once you are clear on what you want to achieve and who you want to influence it is time to begin.

Nothing will improve your storytelling more than practice. Your personal experiences of watching your stories work their magic will be so gratifying that you won't have to remind yourself to include a story—it will become second nature. Initially, you may experience a natural hesitancy due to thoughts that include "I'm not a good storyteller," "This takes too long," "It is unprofessional to share personal anecdotes," or "I have real work to do." These are escape doors to avoid discomfort, uncertainty, and risk. I know all about escape doors. As a writer, my mind offers escape doors like, "Have you checked your e-mails?" or "You should really call X and confirm Y" or "Did you remember to turn the dishwasher on?" and the worst, "I wonder what is in the refrigerator?" At some point you have to decide to just "do it."

In order to jump-start your storytelling practice, Chapters 5 through 10 will protect you from avoidable pitfalls, record what you learn, and accumulate good stories for future use. There is a chapter for each of the six kinds of stories that will give you ample opportunities to practice and cement the principles and philosophical approach that creates good storytelling.

In each chapter you will identify four different story ideas. Develop one of them immediately so you can practice translating an idea into a story, test that story, record your results, and refine your stories. By the end of the exercises you will have incorporated mental habits that make it easy to find, develop, and tell stories whenever you want to win hearts and minds to your point of view.

Where Do I Find Stories?

Researching the Internet, identifying case studies, or current events is a good way to find events that provide examples of your ideas. However, stories are more than mere examples. Winning stories feel personally significant to your listeners. The catch is, only by finding and telling stories that feel personally significant to *you* can you expect to elicit the level of personal engagement that wins hearts and minds. An emotional and thus personal connection to your mutual (as teller/listener) experience of the "example" is what engraves your meaning. When this meaningful point of view is imprinted, future experiences are more likely to flow along the channel of interpretation left by the story.

This is a subtle yet vital distinction often overlooked in "professional" settings. Some people think personal stories are inappropriate. Sure, there is such a thing as too personal—anything that makes people cringe or that generates shouts of "TMI!" (too much information) is too personal. However, in most cases personal stories are always appropriate whenever "persons" are involved.

One advantage of using personal stories is that they are easy to remember. After all, you were there when everything happened. When people ask questions, you can answer them. Curiosity is a vital goal of storytelling and questions often follow a powerful story. If you are telling a story about Lou Gerstner at IBM, you may have trouble answering detailed questions (unless you *are* Lou Gerstner). In order to tell the story you need to know the back story. The amount of research required to know you could answer any questions about a story will make it your story. Your personal version of and response to another person's experience becomes personal enough to make an impact.

Authenticity-in-action means sharing personal stories or personal feelings about someone else's story. Sharing personal experiences earns you trust at the same time you share information or exert influence. To simplify and accelerate your storytelling I present four buckets full of many stories that tell who you are, why you are here, your vision, teaching points, values, and secret empathies. The four buckets are:

1. A time you shined

2. A time you blew it

3. A mentor

4. A book, movie, or current event

These four buckets aren't the only places to find stories, but they may be the easiest. Let's leave it to the academics to pore over sources of plots and perfect arcs, we just need stories that work. As you read the examples for each of these four sources of stories in the next six chapters, jot down as many ideas as pop into your mind. Writing it down is no commitment that you will tell that story in public. Don't be inhibited by second guessing yourself. Coming up with ideas is faster and more creative once you turn the internal editor concerned with appearances OFF and turn the internal compass that tells you who you really are ON. Inauthentic stories only happen when you try to hide who you really are or try to be someone you are not.

The first two buckets are clearly personal stories. These are specifically stories about something that happened to you.

1. *A Time You Shined.* This kind of story is about something good that happened to you. If you are communicating a quality like integrity, a value like compassion, or a learning situation, these stories will tell about a time in your life when it would've been easier to do anything but the "right" thing. All the outside pressures told you to do one thing, but you did the "right" thing and everything turned out for the best. You were being tested and you came through.

2. *A Time You Blew It.* This is about a time when something bad happened and it was all your fault. It sounds backwards, but telling a story that discloses a mistake can increase trust twice

WESTCHESTER LIBRARY CHESTERTON, IN

as fast as polishing the story to give it a professional finish. The very fact that you are sharing a personal failure, flaw, or embarrassing moment means that in the trust dance, you trust them enough to go first. Trust often fails because neither side wants to go first. When you go first you get the ball rolling and people are more likely to trust you back. Don't worry that people will think you are a failure—successful people always have failure stories. This story works because people can tell by the way you tell the story and the tone in your voice how you felt about failing your own standards and how hard you strive to never let it happen again.

3. *A Mentor.* The third kind of story could be personal experiences of an important person in your life, or the personal impact of someone you may have never met. You are sharing an experience or a story that taught you something important in an effort to share the valuable lesson with others. Telling a story of admiration and gratitude toward another person who embodies the qualities or goals you value not only communicates these qualities and goals, it demonstrates to your listener the very important qualities of humility and gratitude. These two qualities are vital in good leadership. Humility and gratitude are the essence of personal dignity. Another advantage in telling a mentor story is that people automatically assume that you share these qualities, values, goals. Particularly when you can't come right out and say, "I'm humble," your stories become clues for others to interpret.

4. *A Book, Movie, or Current Event.* There are millions of stories from books, movies, newspaper articles, or other media sources that might just be perfect to make your point. There are ways to make even these stories personal. Find a scene from a movie, book, or current event that exemplifies what you wish to illustrate. Choosing a well-known book or movie

takes advantage of all the hard work the author or director put into stimulating senses and capturing attention. If you tell a story about the movie *Independence Day*, you don't have to conjure up your own special effects to blow up the White House because the director Roland Emmerich has already done it all for you. Make the story yours by adapting the format and style, including the details of how you came across this story, or by elaborating on what this story has meant to you and why you are sharing it.

These four primary sources for stories are reliable for just about any situation. As you develop as a storyteller you will become aware of your favorite source for stories, and by then you'll have your own methodology. These four buckets will get you started in the meantime.

Getting Feedback

If you are practicing storytelling with a work group or as a part of a training class you have ready listeners handy. If you are doing this alone you will need to find one or more listeners who can resist the urge to "critique" your stories. This sounds wimpy at first—but stay with me. Storytelling is more of an art than a science. The creative process thrives on a mysterious creative force that could be described as "feeling creative," "finding your inspiration," or "being in the flow."

This creative force is a delicate and very subjective process. It's like a timid wild animal you want to tame to eat out of your hand. Loud noises or sudden scary movements scare it off. Over time you can domesticate it to some extent, but part of that process will be feeding it and learning what it likes. I have a writer friend who writes with five sharp number two pencils, and is completely put off if his wife sweeps away the eraser dust. Creativity comes to those who aren't afraid to tune in to their own eccentricities.

Criticism is a tool that improves objective skills, yet it will kill subjective creativity if applied too soon. Professional artists sometimes seem eccentric to us because they have learned that their creative juices flow better with special treatment. Another metaphor that helps me is that a new story must be tended like a new fruit tree is tended by a gardener. The tree needs what it needs when it needs it. And in the beginning the tree needs water and light. It is too soon to prune. Pruning the tree can kill it before it has a chance to grow. Leave it in the dark for too long and it dies. Overwater it and it dies.

Think about your stories in the same way. They are little trees that first need water and light. Criticizing a story too soon just demoralizes the teller and invalidates the subject. Half the time I think criticism is more about the critic than the subject of critique anyway. If you are a perfectly secure, emotionally healthy person who is telling a story that does not carry any strong feelings maybe you want a critique. But please don't let social pressures and ridiculous phrases like, "Don't take this personally" bully you into listening to criticism before your story is strong enough. Storytelling is personal—of course you are going to take it personally. That's why we are doing it: Storytelling brings personal engagement back into our organizations and social interactions.

The word *feedback* (as in "I need to give you some feedback") has become a socially acceptable term in some dysfunctional organizations for what looks remarkably like emotional abuse to me. As long as you make your living doing something other than storytelling, my advice to you is to ask to hear "what works" (this is based on the appreciations model developed by Doug Lipman in his book, *The Storytelling Coach*[1]). Understand that it takes more courage to ask for positive comments than it does to ask for feedback.

I'm not suggesting this method to protect your delicate ego.

I'm suggesting this method because it works. This method encourages the strong parts of your story to grow toward the light. Because it is too soon to prune—negative feedback (I don't care how self-confident you are) kills a baby story because it focuses on the wrong things—literally.

Training a Listener

In order to test your stories you need a listener or listeners. Practicing in a mirror or in the car alone is not good enough. Story is a co-creation in your mind and the mind of at least one listener. It's not storytelling without a listener—it's acting or preaching or something else. Your story should be different every time you tell it, in response to your listener. You can't practice responding to your listener without a live listener.

For your first test-tellings, you'll want a "no-risk" listener. Recruit a best friend, spouse, or coach, who will agree to give you positive feedback (only) for your first telling of any story that you intend to use later in a higher-risk setting. The second telling can be at work or in a "real life" situation, but your first telling needs to be "no risk," so that you can explore the story and develop your skills.

Stories are distorted by premature feedback and suggestions. Sometimes you get negative feedback in the form of, "Can I make a suggestion?" One time I got a "suggestion," and as a result I dropped a detail out of a story when next I told it. The story fell flat without it, so I put that detail back in. I've since come to the conclusion that the person who made the suggestion may have felt judged by his interpretation of what that detail meant. After reflecting, I realized that I wanted this detail to provoke self-examination. I had said, "Nasrudin had not prepared his words to touch the hearts and minds of the people, he thought he could wing it." My choice of wording makes "winging it" sound like an act of hubris. I'm okay with that. If I can save anyone from suffering through unprepared stream-of-consciousness ramblings, it is worth it.

Opening the floor to criticism often gives you more information about your listeners' pet peeves than the quality of your story. Appreciations are much more reliable in finding the parts of your story that work and letting the other parts die on the vine. The secret of good storytelling is having the confidence to protect your creative process in the early stages from criticism—internal as well as external.

Use this format to ask for what works:

"What your story tells me about you is . . ."

"What I like about your story . . ."

"What your story helps me remember . . ."

"The impact I can see your story having in a specific situation (describe) is . . ."

It may feel wimpy asking only for positive feedback, but after a while you will see it actually takes more courage to protect your creative process—courage you can use in other situations to protect good boundaries.

Note

1. Doug Lipman, *The Storytelling Coach* (Atlanta: August House, 1995).

PART TWO

Finding Stories to Tell

CHAPTER 5
Who-I-Am Stories

THE MOST IMPORTANT story you will ever tell is, "Who are you?" Your life is the long version of that story. Everything you have been, done, haven't done, dreamed of, will do, will be, and won't be . . . is your story. Your ability to influence people is directly related to what those people know (or believe) about who you are—you personally and your organization.

Your attempts to influence others are filtered through people's judgments about who you are: your trustworthiness, values, ambitions, and integrity. The disadvantage we all face in today's world is that people actively protect themselves from external influences. Who can blame them? They can't afford to do one more thing today; they don't want to hear of yet another issue that needs their attention or money. In today's world, influence is actively resisted, not only because people are up to their eyeballs in information but because cynicism is justifiably at an all time high.

Chances are that most people would prefer NOT to trust you. If they can treat you as untrustworthy, it makes their life a whole lot easier. So people make up a story (without realizing it) that paints you as "ambitious, or greedy, or inexperienced, or dumb"— anything that justifies not listening. Because listening to you, really listening, might force them to question their current beliefs, change direction, or risk failure.

And lots of times those you wish to influence genuinely *don't* know you. You are a stranger. In the absence of information people always make up a story to protect themselves from yet someone else who wants something. Incomplete stories are automatically untrustworthy. Humans naturally treat incomplete information with wariness. We tend to fill in the blanks with cautionary tales. Think about it. When your boss says, "I need to see you in my office in five minutes," do you make up a good story ("I bet I'm gonna get a raise!") or does your reaction lean more toward an "Oh no, what went wrong now?" direction?

The rational thing would be to wait until you get more information. But humans aren't rational—never have been, never will be. Incomplete information is almost always filled with worst-case-scenario stories. We have to do a better job giving people true stories of good intentions, right actions, and positive outcomes. True stories build faith in us, our leadership, and our future. Faith keeps people doing their best, giving their all, and creatively surviving unavoidable trouble.

People don't want more information. They can't process the information they already have. What they want is faith in you, your words, and your good intentions. We crave personal experiences that build up our faith and if that's not possible we want true stories that feel like personal experiences.

Lucky for us you are a good person—misunderstood maybe, but positively intended. Your job is to break through the worst-case-scenario stories so people can see, at a deeper level, who you really are beneath the surface. This is also called intimacy, so if you are going to break out in hives, do it now. People can't trust someone they don't know. If you are so professional and so private that no one really knows you, you are making it twice as hard for them to trust you.

A *New York Times*/CBS survey (July 1999) asked, "Of people in general, how many do you think are trustworthy?" People averaged out to thinking about 30 percent of people in general would be trustworthy. Then it asked, "Of people *you know,* how many do you think are trustworthy?" The answer? 70 percent. Not only is it statistically impossible for these beliefs to be accurate, but it further demonstrates the irrational (nonlinear!) dynamics of trust. If I feel I know you personally I will attribute twice as much trustworthiness to you. If you are a stranger I give you a 30 percent chance of being trustworthy. When you reveal something personal about yourself people feel they *know* you. Trying to be professional or smooth can come across as cold or too slick. People want you to be real.

Your first step in developing your Who-I-Am story is to answer the questions: Who are you? What makes you special? What earns you the right to influence? Everyone has gifts. What are yours? Are you compassionate, reliable, honest, diplomatic (not usually the same person)? What is it in you that earns you the right to influence others?

Who Are You?

STEP ONE. What qualities earn you the right to influence this person? People want evidence that you have these qualities. Make it personal—trust is always a personal decision. List the qualities that "earn you the right" to influence others (for example, trustworthy, passionate, responsible, creative, compassionate, honest, diplomatic, etc.):

_____

_____

_____

STEP TWO. After you have a list, start looking for stories that demonstrate that quality in a visceral way for your listeners. Give them an experiential sample of this quality so they can decide for themselves from their personal experience that you are trustworthy

Following are examples of Who-I-Am stories from all four buckets. Read each one and immediately take a few minutes to jot down ideas of stories you might develop for telling.

A Time You *Shined*

> I do a lot of pro bono work. A friend and I designed a process called PhotoStory we borrowed from Caroline Wang—who used disposable cameras for poor women in China so they could communicate their needs without English. We adapted it for a community in Houston—poor enough that even pizza delivery men refused to go there. We asked people to use the cameras to tell their story. Telling their story invited the group to examine their story. They had lived with a "Someone ought to do something" story and this process created a "I'm going to do something" story. They said, "It opened our eyes." It opened one woman's eyes enough for her to make big changes. She originally nodded off to sleep in group meetings because she had a morphine pump that treated terrible pain from a botched cancer treatment on her spine. She had given up. Yet this process literally opened her eyes. Three years later I saw her and she had removed the morphine pump and was WIDE awake. She contacted service agencies and rattled the cages of

people who weren't doing their jobs. She now has a computer and is actively developing a community health program. I get energy when I see how story makes people feel more alive, live better, see opportunities they didn't see before. It's what feeds me.

Think of a story that demonstrates one (or more) of the qualities you listed. Perhaps it would have been easier to choose another action or someone tried to persuade you to lighten up just this one time. Think of a time when it cost you something to stand by this quality/value and your behavior demonstrates how important this quality means to you when the chips are down. Or a time when sticking to this value paid off tenfold.

_____

_____

_____

_____

_____

A Time You *Blew It*

Here is an example from my life of a time when I blew it (I have *many* to choose from):

When I first started my consulting business, I landed a very big client. I was still testing ideas, but I didn't want to seem inexperienced. I confess that I had one of those answering machine messages that said, "We can't come to the phone right now" as if I had a whole staff there. I was working out of my house. "We" could only mean me or my dog, Larry. Larry sure as heck wasn't going to answer the phone—even if he'd had opposing thumbs.

Back to the client. I had a process that I had used many times, which I sold to Mark, the VP of Services. He asked me if I could adapt the process to accommodate seventy people. I looked him straight in the eye and said, "Sure." What I didn't explain was that I'd never done it with more than twenty people. Basically the process was to gather and compile customer comments (piece of cake) and then hand out verbatim customer comments for the *team* to analyze. I knew they'd value their own conclusions more than a research company's summary and recommendations. But 70 people agreeing on their interpretations? I designed logistical aids. They were to cut out the most important comments and collectively assemble them on the walls with sticky notes in a way that simultaneously made sense and demonstrated the frequency of recurrence. I assigned different-colored highlighters to mean different things. I thought I had it covered. About halfway through I looked around and one group had stolen all the highlighters to make a tower. Paper was everywhere. It was chaos.

Mark came over and stood beside me rocking once front to back on the balls of his feet. He asked, "You've never done this before, have you?" I said, "Nope." He nodded. "Didn't think so." Then he smiled, handed me a bottle of water, and said, "Thought you might be thirsty," and walked away. God bless his heart.

I'll always remember his kindness. The process wasn't a total disaster—we did get more cohesive action out of those people. But NEVER again! From now on my principle is to undersell and overdeliver, it's better for everyone that way.

Think of a time when you really blew it. A time when you acted out of character to your values. Counterintuitively people will more readily believe you understand the value of a quality when you can accurately tell about paying a price for NOT having this quality.

_____

_____

_____

_____

_____

A *Mentor*

This story is about a mentor I've never met. His name is Antanas Mockus, a past mayor of Bogota. A friend from Colombia told me about the traffic problems they were having in Bogota. The only people that owned cars in Bogota were rich and they thought traffic rules were suggestions. They ran red lights or nudged through pedestrian crossings . . . and people were getting killed. Now imagine what you or I would do to solve this problem. Better enforcement? stiffer penalties? Not Antanas Mockus, he hired mimes. (I'm not making this up.) He hired mimes to monitor the pedestrian crossings and other risky areas. The mimes called attention to any motorist disobeying the rules. They would wag their fingers, signal stop, or call pedestrians over to help train a driver to follow the rules.

And guess what? Pedestrian deaths dropped by more than half. After visiting Bogota, I e-mailed a magazine article I wrote to a guy who worked for the administration named Juan Uribe, and he e-mailed me back: "The way you write the story says that the mimes trained the drivers to obey rules. . . . No, the mimes trained the pedestrians that they had rights." Ohhhh yeah, big difference. That's the kind of work I want to do in the world.

Take some time to reflect. Who taught you about these qualities? It might be a parent or grandparent, maybe even a teacher or scout leader. When you tell a story of the person who exemplified this value, your telling reveals as much about you as it does about the person in your story.

_____

_____

_____

_____

_____

A Book, Movie, or Current Event

When I first developed a training course on storytelling, I used clips from the movie *Amistad*. All of us at one time or another have faced injustice so great that our task has felt impossible. For me the movie *Amistad* is a good example of trying to achieve the impossible—and succeeding.

In the movie *Amistad*, forty-four West Africans snatched from their homes, chained, starved, and beaten, somehow took control of their captors' ship, but were apprehended trying to get home. Can you imagine being their lawyer? Trying to get black men and women justice in a country where slavery is legal, where talk of slavery is about to spark a civil war. The president is up for reelection and would rather not have a civil war. And you are speaking to a jury of twelve white guys, representing forty-four black men and women that don't speak a word of English. That's what I call trying to achieve the impossible. But they won. How? In the movie a grumpy ex-president, John Adams, refusing again to formally help (he eventually joins the fight), gives a frustrated abolitionist a hint, "In a court of law I've found that whoever tells the best story, wins." So they found a translator, learned what happened, and retold their story in a way that was so compelling it outlasted four overturned verdicts. And it turned a handpicked judge, who found them innocent even though it was suicide for his career. Their story was so powerful no one who heard it could deny them the justice they deserved.

Find a book or a movie that tells a good story about this quality. It may only be a scene from a movie, or a snippet from a book. The scenes that stick in your mind, stick in your mind for a reason.

_____

_____

_____

_____

_____

_____

STEP THREE. Choose one of these ideas to develop into a story. Write the story here in your journal. Do not edit. Write in whatever order it comes, including every single detail you can remember. Provide sensory details for all five senses. Write as much as you can remember.

_____

_____

_____

_____

_____

_____

_____

_____

_____

_____

_____

_____

_____

_____

_____

_____

_____

_____

_____

_____

_____

_____

_____

_____

_____

_____

_____

STEP FOUR. Now put your journal away and find someone who will listen to a "test-telling" of this story. Tell your story without these notes (this is storytelling, not story reading!) to someone you trust.

STEP FIVE. Ask your listeners to tell you "what works" in your story. Record the specific things they liked about your story. Record their "take away" from your story—exactly as they reported it.

_____

_____

_____

_____

_____

_____

_____

_____

_____

_____

_____

_____

_____

STEP SIX. Now write your own thoughts about this story. What do you like best? When you tell it again what do you want to remember to say first or last? Are there any new details you can include to make this story more vibrant or alive? Is there a particular order that is more engaging?

_____

_____

_____

_____

_____

_____

_____

_____

_____

_____

_____

_____

_____

_____

_____

_____

_____

_____

_____

_____

_____

_____

_____

CHAPTER 6

Why-I-Am-Here Stories

WHEN YOU ASK people to listen to you, there is a little voice in their heads that wonders, "What's in it for you?" Most people assume if you have taken time, effort, and money to ask them to do something, you are getting something out of it. They don't mind that you get paid to "sell" ideas or products. If you do not earn money out of the deal, they will, with evidence, buy into altruism. Regardless, there is an internal sense of fairness that judges the ratio of what you get out of this exchange in comparison to what they get. Even when people know they can get exactly what they want, they scan the deal for any evidence that you might be using them to get more than your fair share (completely subjective). Any sniff of exploitation from a transaction can be enough for a person to pull the plug on a deal—even if it costs them.

Experimental economics reveals via simulations, such as investment games and public good games, that fairness and reciprocity often matter more than utility. If an offer feels exploitative people prefer to take nothing and will even pay their own money to punish a "free rider." It's very human to abhor a user.

This doesn't mean that the benefits of a product or idea are not important to a prospective buyer, it just means that we need to pay attention to the sequencing of our message. I was taught in Marketing and Sales 101 that answering their WIIFM—"What's In It For ME?"—should be first. And yes, people certainly need to know what's in it for them. However, I've noticed, and you may also have noticed, that people don't relax and listen to what is in it for them until they are satisfied they know what's in it for YOU.

No one wants to feel conned. Big promises of great benefit naturally raise the question: What's in it for you? Turning a profit is fair enough. If everyone at the table is there to make money, and the distribution seems fair, then they are ready to listen to what comes next. However, if your prospect smells a rat, every benefit you promise is sniffed with suspicion.

It's hard to tell if there ever was a deep social shift where "greed is good" was accepted as normal business on a large scale. Whoever tells the best story wins, and during the 1980s there were some master storytellers telling the "greed is good" story. Certainly those in jail or under prosecution for dishonorable business practices bought into that story. I prefer to believe that most people have always had a strong preference for honorable profits. It is to the greater good that we now have better documentation to ensure ethical behavior. The stories of shifty accounting scams at companies like Enron and WorldCom have increased the demand for proof that you and your company operate with integrity and transparency.

The Sarbanes-Oxley rules aren't enough to deliver that warm, safe, trusting feeling to the general public. Most of us in the general public couldn't comprehend the numbers even if we had them, and we simply assume trickery unless proven otherwise. People don't want to see detailed financials. We simply want some kind of experience that makes us feel that you aren't a "user."

When someone recently told me a story about toying with the idea of lying to a police officer about speeding, I immediately assumed the man was fundamentally a truth teller—even when sorely tempted to lie. It was not rational or objective, but when a federal employee told me his story about struggling to tell the truth when asked, "Sir, do you know how fast you were going?" my trust increased. It was something about the way he described looking in his rear view mirror at his four-year-old daughter's eyes knowing she just heard him reassure her mommy, "Relax, I'm only going ten miles over the speed limit."

His desire to be a good dad earns him points with me, because most meetings I attend are full of people who are there primarily to provide a good life for their families. Most humans feel the urge to lie regardless of how smart or stupid it may be. Someone with enough self-awareness and integrity to admit that urge publicly is more trustworthy. I'm more trusting of someone who acknowledges temptation than of anyone who arrogantly purports that he always acts with integrity. His story is a good enough answer to my implicit question, "Why Are You Here?" I interpret his story to answer the question: "I'm here to do the right thing even when I don't want to." Once I know this, I'm ready to listen to what ideas he has to share.

Why Are You Here?

In most purchase decisions people choose to buy from people who are in the business for the love of it as well as the money, over those who are only in it just for the money. When fundraising, "why you are here" is even more important.

Remember, most people automatically assume you are selling something they don't really want or need, some idea that will increase the number of things they have to do today, or some other self-serving sneakiness that will benefit you more than them. This is perfectly normal. Our suspicions protect us from being duped, but it also unfairly discredits others as biased. Unless it is true that you seek only personal gain, you must take time to tell them why you are there. If you do seek only personal gain you need to work on more than just your story. The life of a user is a lonely life.

Most of us only need to let others know what makes us passionate about this deal, sale, or idea. Think about what gives you a deep sense of fulfillment: past successes of clients, the enjoyment of watching your client discover a new idea, the pleasure of a good night's sleep knowing you helped someone.

STEP ONE. Think about the last time someone said "thank you" for a job well done. Why ARE you there trying to persuade people? Sure you get something for yourself, but surely you have other reasons, too. List some of them here.

_____

_____

_____

STEP TWO. After you have examined "why" you do what you do, start looking for stories that demonstrate in a visceral way the benefits you seek. Give your listeners an experiential sample of the charge you get from success so they can decide for themselves from their personal experience if you really are here for the right reasons.

Following are examples of Why-I-Am-Here stories from all four buckets. Read each one and immediately take a few minutes to jot down ideas of stories you might develop for yourself.

A Time You *Shined*

I was hired by a group of military decision makers to help facilitate a budget meeting. Their budgets had been cut about 15 percent every year for three years. For the previous three years the group had left planning meetings with action plans and good intentions to cut services in proportion to budget cuts. For three years decisions were overturned, ignored, or weakened by critical events. The group had not succeeded in making any substantial cuts. They were still doing everything they did three years ago with fewer and fewer resources. They were squeezed so tight everyone was frustrated and some were downright angry. Blame was starting to seep into e-mails, and the group was poised for a show-down. Budget meetings were typically considered a battleground anyway, so the atmosphere was emotionally tense, suspicious, and cynical.

So, I used poetry. Yep. I have no fear. I said, "We need to talk about feelings before we get to the numbers." I talked really fast before they could kick me out. "I want to draw your attention to the feeling state that wins a war, and then we will examine the feeling state that helps you make good decisions about allocating resources.

"Let's examine the feeling state that wins a war first," I said. "I'd like to read part of a speech from Shakespeare's *Henry V*":

> "*Once more unto the breach, dear friends, once more;*
> *Or close the wall up with our English dead.*
> *In peace there's nothing so becomes a man*
> *As modest stillness and humility:*
> *But when the blast of war blows in our ears,*
> *Then imitate the action of the tiger;*
> *Stiffen the sinews, summon up the blood,*
> *Disguise fair nature with hard-favour'd rage.*"

By the time I finished they were hulked into body-builder poses doing the Tim Allen grunt, "H-o-o-Ho-o-Ho-o." I said, "This is how you work up a group to win a war with speed and aggression. This emotional state evokes specific behaviors, like surprise attacks, diversion, and secrecy. But we aren't here to fight a war. We are here to make sober, calm budget decisions. This next poem describes the emotional state from which we can make wise, more considered decisions. This emotional state inspires very different behaviors."

Then I read from Billy Rose's poem, "The Unknown Soldier":

"I am the Unknown Soldier,"
The spirit voice began,
"And I think I have the right
To ask some questions man to man.

"Are my buddies taken care of?
Was their victory so sweet?
Is that big reward you offered
Selling pencils on the street?

"Did they really win the freedom
They battled to achieve?
Do you still respect that Croix de Guerre
Above that empty sleeve?

I asked them "Can you feel the difference?" You could have heard a pin drop. Then I suggested they each know at least one person they had lost in a war situation. "If that man or woman could speak from the grave right now, what would they ask you to remember? What would they tell you to forget?"

These two story/poems changed the emotional climate of the people in the room. Frustration turned to courage, anger to resolve, and arrogance to humility. The conversations they had and the decisions they made were much more collaborative and more firmly grounded. Explaining why I was there caused them to reflect on why they were there.

We all have some idea of "doing the right thing for the right reasons." Think back to a time when you felt like you did the right thing for the right reasons. Or even the "wrong thing" for the right reasons. Life is so complex, these kinds of stories aren't often told because it feels so risky to discuss a moral judgment that may (probably will) contradict common wisdom or other people's opinions. However, sharing a risky story about "Why You Are Here" anchors trust in a visceral way—even if your listener might have chosen another option. The point is that you both struggled over a moral dilemma. Think of a time you delivered more than people expected—a time when it would have been more to your personal advantage to walk away, but you didn't because you wanted to take care of your client, coworker, boss, employee, or someone else important:

_____

_____

_____

_____

_____

A Time You *Blew It*

One of my all time favorite self-disclosure stories was told by a very dignified senior partner of a big accounting firm—one of the big four. (Remember when there were eight?) They hired me to teach storytelling to increase clients' feelings of trust toward their firm. When the time came to share stories in a room of 150 partners, not one person was willing to risk going first—which tells you a bit about trust *inside* that firm. After a long wait, one of the most respected and powerful men in the room stood and walked to the front. He said:

> "I had a really good day last month. My team was play-
> ing and I was there, watching from the 50-yard line. We
> won the game. I was a happy man. I went back to my
> hotel room. I ordered a cheeseburger, fries, and two
> beers. After room service delivered it, in order to prop-
> erly enjoy my feast, I stripped down to my tighty whi-
> ties. I ate every bit of it. (Big smile) Lordy, I was a
> happy man. Until I went to set my tray outside and the
> napkin caught the glass and when I reached to catch it,
> I heard the click.
>
> "I guess I should've realized there would be people
> on the elevator. But when it opened I did a little left-
> right-left look before I decided to hide behind a nearby
> palm tree. After that I punched the button and hid until
> I finally got an empty elevator. On my way down I real-
> ized I would soon have another problem. (Pause) I de-
> cided speed would be my friend so I streaked across the
> lobby. Halfway across I heard someone at the desk yell
> out, 'What number?' I told them, grabbed my new card
> key, ran back. When I was safe in my room, out of
> breath from my adventure, the phone rang. I puffed out,
> 'Hello?' This sweet voice said, 'Sir, we just wanted you
> to know, if this ever happens again, we have phones on
> every floor.'"

The group was still laughing when he sat down. His story told the group, "I'm here to learn and have fun. I'm willing to embarrass myself to do it." Once they heard his story almost everyone else decided that was why they were there as well.

Think about a time you caved in and regretted your action. Or perhaps there was a situation where you made a mistake, could have hidden it, but didn't. Big mistakes make fabulous stories as long as you aren't telling about unfinished issues. This is not the place to purge old shame and clean out an old skeleton for the first time. However, if you are emotionally finished with an issue, and have tested the skeleton for reactions, it's a great time to turn a mistake into a good story. Particularly if you suspect someone might use this mistake against you.

When you tell a "mea culpa" story about your own mistakes first, it cheats your adversaries of the opportunity to discredit your intentions and polishes your reputation for transparency at the same time. Everyone has a time when they abused their influence for their own gain. Either out of greed, ambition, or insecurity you cut corners or put your own gain before your principles. Tell about a time when you forgot "why" you were there and tell the story in a way so people see that you will never let that happen again:

A *Mentor*

One of my mentors was a man named Jim Farr. He always said, "A difference to be a difference must make a difference." By the time I met him he had been a practicing psychologist for forty-five years, teaching leadership for twenty-five years. He was 75 at the time—loving, compassionate, and brilliant, rolled up into one grumpy package. Jim didn't tiptoe around the truth. He told it like it was. Those of us who worked for him teased that he was "lovingly abusive." He could work you over—that's for sure. Jim was a 7th-level black belt in Aikido (a martial art dedicated to avoiding a fight or ending a fight quickly with least effort). In Aikido when someone comes after you, the idea is to tap into their momentum, turn their direction, bring them close and whomp, turn their attack into a little face time with the floor. Jim did this mentally as well as physically.

One day, he was trying to explain to me how much energy I wasted struggling against the flow. It seems my constant search for improvement had been reported by my peers as constant criticism—go figure. I must have been driving everyone nuts. He stood up, motioned for me to stand, and said, "throw me a punch." I stuck my fist out in my best impression of a punch, and two seconds later I was on the floor. I was a fit 32 years old at the time, and he was 77. Then he did it again in slow motion. I threw the punch, and instead of punching me back he took my "offered" fist and pulled me toward him stepping left. He kept pulling until my body followed the momentum my punching arm had started. I was on the floor . . . again. He asked, "Now do you get it?"

I'll never forget him, or that moment. He taught me that throwing a punch is not always an "attack." It can also be an invitation to turn in that person's direction and see what they see. At that point I can stop and look, or keep the momentum swinging back around to my point of view. It doesn't work all the time, but at least I know from now on that I have many responses from which to choose when I feel attacked or feel like attacking what I see as a mistake. I don't have to respond at all. If someone wants to win, I can let them. I'm here to learn, not debate.

People rarely have long conversations about "why" we are here. But if you reflect back, you will find one or two people who inspired you by their example. They may even have done something that literally made it possible for you to get to where you are. Tell a story about that person most responsible for you choosing this path. What person comes to your mind when you think about why you are here? What historical figure comes to mind as a role model for going the extra mile, not cutting corners, remembering the bigger picture? Who is that person? What story can you tell about how they inspire you to remember why you are here?

A *Book, Movie, or Current Event*

A manager of a large retail company found himself with really bad numbers to report at the next sales meeting of over 2,000 sales staff members. Due to economic conditions, their last year's performance was terrible. They had done the best they could but they had still failed their own goals. He chose to reframe facing that "failure" as heroic rather than weakness by using a scene from the film, *The Matrix*. In *The Matrix*, which is a movie about choices, an underground operative has powerful information that will change the neophyte from amateur into a warrior for justice. Accepting the responsibilities of knowing this information takes courage—it is a tough road. Morpheus forces Neo to understand that knowledge and wisdom can be a bitter pill to swallow, so he offers Neo a choice between a red pill or a blue pill. The manager retells the scene:

> **Morpheus** (with a blue pill in his hand): "You take the blue pill and the story ends. You wake up in your bed and believe whatever you want to believe. (A red pill is now shown in his other hand.) You take the red pill and I show you how deep the rabbit-hole goes."

> **Neo** thinks long and hard. Ignorance is bliss, right? He starts to reach for the red pill.

> **Morpheus**: "Remember, all I am offering is the truth, nothing more."

The manager continues: "So that's what my presentation delivers. Denial or a positive spin would be easier. We have some tough choices to make. This data I'm about to show you is a red pill. But I'd rather deal with the truth. What about you? Do you want the red pill (the truth) or you want me to blow blue smoke?"

Of course the entire auditorium erupted in calls for the truth. This story not only told a compelling Why-I-Am-Here story, it reframed bad news as a courageous act. Good storytelling.

Again, with a movie the special effects are already there, talent has been paid, all you need to do is describe a scene that brings it back to life. I like books even more. John Steinbeck is one of my all time favorite authors because he tells the "whole story." Steinbeck includes all of what is good and what is terrible about human nature, and at the end you miraculously are still glad to be alive. A scene from Steinbeck brings authenticity that never smacks of overoptimistic, upbeat perkiness. Borrowing "old soul" wisdom from this kind of gritty realism lends gravitas, which delivers credibility to your words.

Is there one book or movie that exemplifies the big "why" for you? It may have nothing to do with this particular situation but it inspired you to be a better person. Any movie or book that inspires you will inspire others when you tell the story in a way that reveals the essence of your "inspirational" experience of that story.

_____

_____

_____

_____

_____

_____

Okay . . . now it's your turn.

STEP THREE. Choose one of these ideas to develop into a story. Write the story here in your journal. Do not edit. Write in whatever order it comes, including every single detail you can remember. Provide sensory details for all five senses. Write as much as you can remember:

_____

_____

_____

_____

_____

STEP FOUR. Now put your journal away and find someone who will listen to a "test-telling" of this story. Tell your story without these notes (storytelling, not story reading!) to someone you trust.

STEP FIVE. Ask your listeners for appreciations. Ask them to respond to your story with any of the following appreciation statements, and record what they say:

"What I like about your story is . . .

"What your story tells me about you is. . . .

"The difference hearing your story might make to our working relationship is . . . "

"I can see you using this story when (client situation) in order to (impact) . . . "

_____

_____

_____

_____

_____

_____

_____

_____

_____

_____

_____

_____

_____

_____

STEP SIX. Now write your own thoughts about this story. What do you like best? When you tell it again, what do you want to remember to say first or last? Are there any new details you can include to make this story more vibrant or alive? Is there a particular order that is more engaging?

_____

_____

_____

_____

_____

_____

_____

_____

_____

_____

_____

_____

_____

_____

_____

_____

_____

_____

_____

_____

_____

_____

CHAPTER 7

Teaching Stories

TEACHING IS A SPECIAL kind of influence. The six stories overlap—each emphasizes different aspects of influence but they all do a little bit of everything. A Teaching story can reveal a little bit about who you are and why you are here simply by your choice of material. Yet it's useful for us to treat Teaching stories as a distinct specialty. For our purposes, teaching is about changing behavior and building skills to creatively interpret tasks and goals.

At its best, a Teaching story transports your listener into an experience that lets him or her feel, touch, hear, see, taste, and smell excellent performance. It demonstrates in the mind how new behaviors create new results. A Teaching story is a no-risk demonstration—a trial run by imagination. Scrooge's ghosts were basically taking Scrooge on Teaching-story tours. Each ghost told a different Teaching story, allowing Scrooge to emotionally and mentally experience the subjective consequences of not changing his behavior.

STORY ONE: In your past, you delayed your marriage to make more money and lost Belle, your one true love.

STORY TWO: Your need for money is creating poverty for the Cratchit family.

STORY THREE: Your continued need for money will kill the Cratchits' son, and you will die alone and miserable.

It was a three-story transformation delivered in one night. These experiences delivered in story form are much more effective than scolding or preaching.

Teaching stories travel in time and perspective to enhance your listeners' experiences and thus conclusions about what is the right or smart thing to do here. Highly specific rules and procedures often frighten staff into following these rules and procedures to the letter, regardless of the circumstances. Yet, some of the worst treatment of customers has been perpetrated by "Sorry, I don't make the rules" or "That's not my job" justifications. True customer service is flexible and even breaks the rules on occasion. If a good customer returns an obviously faulty product on the 31st day when you have a 30-day return policy, you want your staff to make an allowance. They need to have the freedom to do the right thing. Rules keep them from making judgment calls. Story gives both room for judgment calls and guidelines for making good judgments.

A casualty of overdoing clarity is the mindless attempt to force good intentions onto grocery story clerks with scripts for greeting customers. Increased clarity in this case actually degrades customer relations. When I reach the register in the supermarket line I feel sorry for the guy or gal who is forced to ask me "Did you find everything you need?" First of all, what if I said "no"? Should the five people behind me stand and wait while I explain that I was looking for gnocchi—which I know darn well they stopped stocking two months ago? Not only is this question badly timed but the person asking it is limited in her ability to do anything about it.

I've never heard anyone say "no." The bosses who make them say it—who would probably penalize them in some way if they didn't say it—have lost faith in the clerk's ability to properly greet customers and otherwise tend to the customer/employee relationship. The clerk knows she isn't trusted to choose her own greeting and has no choice but to decrease her personal engagement in the interchange. She becomes a robot, mechanically polite but less alive and stripped of spontaneity.

Treating a customer well is not predictable enough to handle via objective criteria. It's too subjective. My good friend Pam Mc-Grath, a minister, preached a sermon on "evangelism" that begins with a scene in a grocery story checkout line. She tells it like this:

> A woman and her children are grocery shopping after work on a Friday. The store is fraught with danger: giant cereal boxes, bags of candy, etc. The woman is at wit's end, and just as she finally makes her way to the head of the line at the checkout, the machine runs out of tape. She is impatiently tapping her foot while the kids grab things from the confined area. The checkout girl is trying to hurry. Everyone in the line behind her is sighing. Then she notices the checkout girl has on a cross like her mom used to wear. She says, "Nice cross." The checkout girl stops and looks into her eyes. They smile. She continues, "My mother used to have one like that." The checkout girl says, "My mom gave me this one." They both breathe and smile. Two humans take the opportunity to connect and feel human again.

The kindness of seeing someone—truly noticing their presence with your full attention—is the spirit of customer service. Clearly defining roles and responsibilities to the point of providing "scripts" to people can shut them down. Improving performance may actually occur with fewer lines of demarcation so that staff step into the gray areas and use their imagination to solve problems.

Teaching stories provide a demonstration of how different behaviors yield different results. Some stories will rewind a past action to view it from another point of view. For instance, if you were training a new "caregiver" at a nursing home, it would be wonderful if you could put that strong 24-year-old person into an 87-year-old body for one day—just one day—so he can feel the vibrations of Parkinson's disease distort his ability to walk or sit still. He could feel what it is like to be dependent, and how belittling it feels to have someone say, "And how are we today?" in a singsong voice normally reserved for toddlers. That personal experience would stay with him forever. But we haven't figured out how to switch bodies yet, so the next best thing is to bring life-altering experiences to those who can benefit from Teaching stories.

Certain lessons can only be learned from experience. Some lessons apparently have to be learned over and over again for the rest of our lives. Patience, for instance. You could teach yourself and those around you about patience, using a different story every week, and not overdo it in most cases. What we tend to overdo is repeat unhelpful phrases like "Be more patient" or "I should be more patient." These well-intended reminders don't translate into real live patience when you need it. Nagging like this can do more harm than good.

Patience is one of many skills that combine temperament, experience, intention, and your subjective frame of reference. When you frame issues in a "big picture" frame you have more patience. Thinking in a small picture frame, "I'm late for work" might prompt a snippy "not now" response to your two-year-old's silly question. A big picture frame like, "I'm teaching my two-year-old about the value of curiosity" may generate much more patience. Skill-based training can teach a student "what" patience is, and still miss the "why" or "how."

Whether you are a boss training employees, a parent training teenagers, or a customer training a supplier, a Teaching story better motivates creative interpretations of the spirit of the relationship. When both parties focus on the spirit of the intent they invent innovative ways to meet genuine needs. Using story in teaching situations keeps everyone aware that circumstances change and we need to pay attention to those changes.

When a simple task isn't being done well or is not done with the "spirit" you'd like to see, ask yourself if there might be a compounding problem of resentment or disillusionment. If so, you can bet a story will improve performance. However, remember that you need to start with your Who-I-Am or Why-I-Am-Here story first. The people you want to teach may have been treated like they can't think for themselves for a long time. They may expect more of the same from you. Set things up for success by telling your Who-I-Am or Why-I-Am-Here story before you move into Teaching stories.

One caveat for using story to teach: Remember, it only works 50–70 percent of the time. That's the price you pay for creative interpretation. People miss the mark sometimes. That means that when you inspire and encourage people to think for themselves, they will think for themselves. You must have a correlate norm (and stories) that demonstrate how to report mistakes early, ask forgiveness, and grant forgiveness, even as mistakes are fixed.

Don't use story for everything. Technical issues still need rules and policies. Keep worst-case-scenario-derived rules and procedures for life-and-death situations. Hospital staff requires clarity for technical issues like attaching IVs, but teaching staff about empathy by telling a story of a nurse calming a frightened patient does not require clear policy guidelines. Tasks that require technical proficiency are still best handled with rules and clarity. Yet even technical tasks can be reinforced with stories to illustrate worst-case scenarios in a way that engraves the importance of inflexible perfection on a trainee.

STEP ONE. Now it's time to think about the skills you want to teach others. Start with the basics. Identify a few basic tasks that need improvement. Perhaps you are teaching someone to do your job so you can move up. Consider the deliverables of your job and then move back upstream to consider what you actually do to deliver results. Frequently, your "best skills" are not adequately described with bullet points or summaries. Consider ambiguous situations where you imagine that staff might need to come up with creative solutions. One idea is to simply list your top five pet peeves. If they are pet peeves, it's a good indication that what you have been doing isn't working.

_____

_____

_____

STEP TWO. After you have examined "why" you do what you do, start looking for stories that demonstrate in a visceral way the benefits you seek. Here are four Teaching stories from our four buckets to get your juices flowing with ideas:

A Time You *Shined*

There are many courses on cultural sensitivity. If you had enough time to get a master's degree or a Ph.D. in "cultural differences," you could list thousands of specific ways to offend people in different cultures, such as showing the soles of your feet in an Arab country, or pointing with your index finger in India, and so on. Yet, ultimately the most important skill to learn is constant sensitivity to subjective interpretations that don't match your expectations.

The generalized skill of staying open to new experiences is best taught through stories like this one told by a young lady named Cindy (quite young to me . . . under 25), who had just come back from two years in the Peace Corps. She told about being stationed in the Philippines. Her tour of duty began with a week in the home of a resident of the area. She explained to us that she expected it to be similar to traveling with the church choir back home—prearranged and structured. Instead she stood in a line as she and her new Peace Corps buddies were "sort of auctioned off." Individuals or families arrived, picked out the volunteer they wanted, and led them out the door. The lady who picked her did not speak English. Cindy didn't speak Tagalog. Her advisor assured her she should follow the woman and come back in a week. So she did. This is her story:

> She took me further and further away from clean streets and houses with walls. The regular houses stopped and in their place were tarps on frames, lean-tos, and cardboard boxes. Finally, we arrived at a lean-to right next to the town dump. There were no walls. The floor was the dirt on the ground. I wasn't disgusted so much as . . . well, I was scared. There were bugs everywhere. But I put on a brave face and I helped where I could. We went to get some food and prepared it on an outdoor fire. We ate dinner. I didn't eat much. I didn't feel so good. It got dark. I needed to go to the bathroom but didn't see a bathroom. I didn't see a latrine. I mean I wasn't looking for a tiled floor or a door that said "Ladies." I knew it would be basic, but I literally could not figure it out. I tried to watch to see what others did, but I still didn't know where in the world they went when they needed to "go."
>
> I couldn't ask because I didn't speak the language. Finally, it got urgent. I needed to go, so I had to mime to the lady who was my host. Luckily, a knock-kneed bouncing seems to be the international symbol of "I

need to go." She laughed and laughed and then she showed me in mime that they did number one in a corner nearby in the dirt. Then she began to mime how to handle number two. She took a plastic grocery bag and indicated that you use the bag as a toilet and she handed me the bag, but I was still confused. What would I do with the bag when I was done? She could see my confusion and smiled, took the bag and pretended to swing the bag over her head like a shot put, and hurled it off in the direction of the dump, speaking the only two English words I heard the whole week, "Flying Saucer!"

That story cracked us up. There were 250 people in the room and the phrase "flying saucer" became a code word for how to deal with tough situations. This story is specific to the Philippines and yet useful to any group hoping to help strangers.

Describe a task that has been done by you, your team, or your organization the "right way." Think about a time when the circumstances were confusing and yet the solutions applied were creative and well done. When was it difficult to find a path to solve an internal problem but you came through with flying colors? Certainly, there have been tough times recently that stretched your ability to do a good job. Think about an event or a customer who tempted you to hide behind rules or stock standard answers but instead you invented a solution where none existed before. Or, tell about a time when following a rule you didn't understand ended up saving the situation, client, or even a life. Rules make more sense and are more easily remembered in the context of a Teaching story.

_____

_____

_____

A Time You *Blew It*

I found this story in the *New York Times* nine months after the Space Shuttle Columbia disaster, in which all crew members died. You know part of the story already:

> When the Columbia took off a piece of foam broke off the wing, and without it, the craft burned up on reentry over Texas on February 1, 2003. With the 20/20 hindsight of an in-depth investigation, it was discovered that the data that predicted this disaster was available but was buried deep inside a PowerPoint slide. Edward Tufte, a professor from Yale who specializes in the visual presentation of data, analyzed the slide. The information was in the last line of a nineteen-line slide and read: "Flight condition is significantly outside test database, volume of ramp is 1920 cu. in. vs. 3 cu. in. for test." Much has been made of the visual insignificance of "significantly" relevant data. But more importantly, this story highlights how words on a screen don't deliver enough context to interpret the data's meaning in terms of human life.
>
> The data was there—the piece that broke off in the test was hundreds of times larger than anything they'd ever tested to be safe. But it was out of context. Could lives have been saved with a metaphor like "similar to losing the door panel of your car?" Did PowerPoint kill those people? No. Ted Simons, editor of online magazine *Presentations,* coined the headline, "PowerPoint doesn't kill presentations, people do." My main concern

is that PowerPoint lets you think you communicated when you didn't.

There was a cartoon in the *New Yorker*—a scene from Hell's HR headquarters, where a recruiter for Hell is interviewing a new torturer. The recruiter leans back from his desk and looks at the prospect and asks, "That's all fine and good but do you know PowerPoint?" One of my friends told me that a senior manager is known as "PowerPoint Bob" by his staff, and they don't mean it as a compliment. Trust me, no one will ever complain if you delete a few PowerPoint slides from your presentation and tell a story instead. And depending on what industry you are in . . . you might save a life!

Think of a time your naïveté created a big problem for the customer—specifically a time when following the rules to the letter didn't serve the customer or the organization. Borrow from Dickens and tell three stories of past, present, and future consequences for missing the mark. Disaster stories are sometimes told only to show how stupid someone was or how incompetent people can be. We need to move into a frame of reference where we acknowledge that smart people make mistakes too, and use these mistakes as learning opportunities. In order to sound sincere—use your own mistakes whenever possible. By doing this, you model self-examination and encourage others to self-examine. When did you not follow the rules (in a technical situation) or when did you not break the rules (in an adaptive situation) in a way that you interpret as a mistake?

_____

_____

_____

_____

_____

A *Mentor*

People complain these days about a lack of civility. One hospital group I work with launched an initiative to improve civility, and lo and behold it improved safety performance. Incivility operates like a contagious virus. When one person treats an employee badly, they are more likely to dump on a customer or patient who is usually rude in return. It's a terrible spiral. We parrot the words, "The customer is always right," but that's not true up to 50 to 70 percent of the time. Because it is subjective. If this hard line is held, employees end up feeling abused because no one ever acknowledges how hard it is to be nice to an unpleasant client or patient. Here's a story from a woman in one of my classes who has become a role model for me when I feel mistreated. I try to remember her story because, most of the time, it inspires a creative, even humorous response when I feel like punching someone in the nose or bursting into tears. She told it without a trace of bitterness or self pity:

> I was the ugly girl in high school. As an adult, I now know that every class has one. Your class had an "ugly girl." That was me. I was the one who had cooties in grade school, the freak who was picked last in gym, and in high school there was a group of boys who made my life a living hell. No matter where I hid they'd find me. After school I'd hang back or find a bench far away from the rest of the kids where I waited on my mother to pick me up. I was as invisible as I could be. Thank goodness I didn't have to ride a bus. Anyway, those boys would eventually find me no matter where I hid. When they found me they'd start to play one of their favorite games. One of them would sit beside me, put his arm around me, and they'd all laugh as he'd pretend to ask me out on a date, beg me for a kiss. I would try not to cry but

my chin would start to quiver. The more I cried the more they laughed. This went on for most of a year. Then one day . . . I have *no* idea what came over me. One of these boys had his arm around me, taunting me . . . and something—not really me—but something lifted my left arm and draped it right back over his shoulder. My arm gave him a squeeze. And my brain kicked in and I winked at him. Now the other boys weren't laughing at me anymore, they were laughing at him. I air kissed him and I started to laugh too. I wish you could've seen his face; it was pretty funny.

From that day on things were different. Sure they still teased me, but I never again let myself feel so devastated. I had power and I used it.

It is an old but excellent strategy: Find someone who is successful and copy them. When you adopt the habits, mannerisms, and daily goals of a successful person, you often can recreate their results. Find someone who has the skills you want—study their story and tell their story. For instance, Ben Franklin invented a system to rate himself everyday on the values he chose as important, choosing one a week for special emphasis. Actively seek mentors whose examples inspire you and you will learn things you didn't even know you needed to learn. Autobiographies are an excellent way to study what attitudes, skills, and habits create the kind of life you seek. The beauty of real live mentors is that they have real-life flaws and can teach you how to cope and compensate as well as how to "achieve results." If you don't have mentors, you are wasting a lot of energy reinventing the wheel. Whom did you last witness performing a task in a way that inspired you? Tell about that moment (it could be from work, church, or the Olympics):

_____

_____

_____

_____

_____

A *Book, Movie, or Current Event*

An old friend of mine is a therapist. To keep his license he must constantly earn education credits by attending courses on the latest developments in mental health. He frequently attends free trainings produced by the pharmaceutical industry to keep abreast of the drugs out there and to fulfill his licensing requirements. Sometimes, I like to go too, because I learn more about neuroscience, emotions, and mental health.

The presenters vary considerably in quality. They are all smart. Most have M.D. or Ph.D. degrees, but only a few are interesting to listen to. One psychiatrist stood out for me when he used a story from a movie. Right in the middle of a deck of PowerPoint slides, with graphs of experiments on treating manic depression, I could feel my eyes glazing over as I tried to deal with unfamiliar words like Lamotrigine and Carbamazepine, but I woke up when I heard him say:

> We forget how inexact this science it. You know, it's only fifty years since we discovered lithium. I just read about a movie being produced about John Cade. John Cade, an Australian, discovered the use of lithium for mania in 1947. That was only fifty years ago. At that time everyone else was using electric shock and lobot-

omy, and this Australian doctor—John Cade—started wondering if manic behavior might be a result of too much of something. Maybe the body was intoxicating itself with some internally produced stimulant. He treated ten manic patients at a nearby institution. So he started collecting their urine and feeding it to guinea pigs. Nothing happened. He decided to inject it in the guinea pigs. In order to do that he needed a salt combination as a base fluid. Through trial and error he discovered that lithium carbonate was very stable. He injects it and notices the mixture has a strong sedating effect, which is the very opposite of his theory. Curious enough, he tries it on himself to see if it is safe enough to try it on a patient.

He knew which patient he wanted to treat first—a terribly manic man who was bouncing off the walls. This man's mania was so bad that he had lost his job and was institutionalized. Almost immediately after the injection, the manic man was "more settled, tidier, able to pay attention and to control his impulses." After two weeks of injections the man was able to leave the institution and go back to work. It was a miracle.

John Cade discovered the miracle fifty years ago, and *we still don't know why it works.* (The psychiatrist then paused and looked up at his graphs in silence.)

You can bet we hung on every word he had to say next about his research.

Movies are wonderful for teaching situations. They provide ambiguity that encourages curiosity and discussion. There aren't many human issues that haven't been covered in one way or another by a movie. The classic, *To Kill a Mockingbird,* could stand up to high school students (a tough crowd) even today as a story that prompts introspection about racism, integrity, humility, and stereotyping. List your favorite movies, then write beside each movie title a notation of a scene that stands out as clever, innovative, or simply memorable. Don't worry about the application of this story yet. Work it up as a story by writing the bare skeleton of what happened. Then look at the elements of the story and decide whether these same elements might work as a Teaching story.

Look to books or movies to find a historical character that teaches your point, or one who simply livens up your presentation (e.g., rewrite a *Stripes*-inspired marching chant, characterize a problem using a scene from *Caddyshack*, or adapt a Monty Python skit).

_____

_____

_____

_____

_____

_____

STEP THREE. Choose one of these ideas to develop into a story. Write the story here in your journal. Do not edit. Write in whatever order it comes, including every single detail you can remember. Provide sensory details for all five senses. Write as much as you can remember.

_____

_____

_____

_____

_____

_____

_____

_____

_____

_____

_____

_____

_____

_____

_____

_____

_____

_____

_____

_____

_____

_____

_____

_____

_____

_____

_____

_____

STEP FOUR. Now put your journal away and find someone who will listen to a "test-telling" of this story. Tell your story without these notes (storytelling, not story reading!) to someone you trust.

STEP FIVE. Ask your listeners for appreciations. Ask them to respond to your story with any of the following appreciation statements, and record what they say:

"What I like about your story is . . .

"What your story tells me about you is. . . .

"The difference hearing your story might make to our working relationship is . . ."

"I can see you using this story when (client situation) in order to (impact) . . ."

_____

_____

_____

_____

_____

_____

_____

_____

_____

_____

_____

_____

_____

STEP SIX. Now write your own thoughts about this story. What do you like best? When you tell it again, what do you want to remember to say first or last? Are there any new details you can include to make this story more vibrant or alive? Is there a particular order that is more engaging?

_____

_____

_____

_____

_____

_____

_____

_____

_____

_____

_____

_____

_____

_____

CHAPTER 8

Vision Stories

WHEN I WAS a kid my mother taught me table manners by suggesting I'd need them "in case the queen ever invites you to tea." I'm over 45 and so far I've received no royal invitations, but I do have lovely table manners (as do all of my mother's past fifth-grade students). The Queen's tea party was my mother's version of a Vision story. When you are ten, using a short fork for salad is ridiculous without the "You'll thank me some day" story. Unpleasant chores, training, routine maintenance, disruptive changes in procedure usually offer little immediate gratification. Frustrations experienced in the here and now are borne only because we can imagine the payoff somewhere, sometime in the future. A good Vision story makes otherwise ambiguous promises for future payoffs come alive with carefully crafted sights, sounds, smells, tastes, and feelings that eclipse the work we do today for tomorrow's payoff. Overwhelming obstacles shrink to bearable frustrations that are worth the effort.

A Vision story raises your gaze from current difficulties to a future payoff that successfully competes with the temptation to give up, compromise, or change direction. Without a visceral and easily remembered vision of why in the hell we ever wanted to do this in the first place, it is easy to forget. A Vision story casts the future, just like a bright shiny bicycle in a store window might motivate a child. The child rummages through trash for bottles and cans, baby-sits little monsters, and even washes his parent's station wagon with only a daily glimpse of that bright shiny future. When we see, taste, touch, smell, and hear a shiny future, nothing feels too menial or difficult.

The word "vision" has been distorted for many of us by bad experiences of smarmy consultants, endless management retreats, and oversold and underdelivered promises. Story forces substance back into the vision process. Laminated cards with core values and quippy "$2 billion by 2010" sound-bite visions are exposed as superficial and one-dimensional when compared to Vision stories. When you apply the discipline of interpreting any vision by way of a story, the process inevitably exposes any gaping holes that beg the questions: What does this mean? To whom? And who benefits if I get there? Exploitation, superficiality, and unintended outcomes are more likely to be exposed by the rigors of storytelling.

Vision stories demand a lot, but they deliver a lot too. Scenario planning is a popular application of storytelling to vision. Future goals are interpreted through various scenarios in a narrative simulation of several possible futures. Goals are subjected to reality tests of the imagination through realistically possible future stories. Scenario planning is more "reality based" than more objective strategic planning methods. The critical difference is that your presence is required. Subjective contexts, emotionally stimulated responses, and nonlinear changes are more predictable when smart people take the time to "live the story" in their mind's eye. You can't imagine the future unless "you go there."

It works because at an imagined sensory level you go "there" to the future(s) so you experience places and times intimately enough to play out the possibilities. Walking around in the virtual reality of a story often identifies otherwise unpredictable implications, consequences, and correlating factors that are only visible when imagining specific times and places set in a reality-based story.

The "failure of imagination" implicated as a hole in U.S. domestic security by the 9/11 Commission is a good example of the limitations of objective strategic planning. Think of a Vision story as subjective strategic planning. Vision stories are successes of the imagination. Scenario planning is one type of Vision storytelling. Shell Oil's use of scenario planning led them, decades ago, to see South Africa's apartheid as bad for business (in addition to being morally wrong). They constructed several scenarios of a post-apartheid South Africa, but none of them "felt" possible without an unquestionably ethical leader, ideally home grown.

Shell certainly didn't invent Nelson Mandela. Yet, thinking about the Shell scenario-planning team I have to wonder whether you and I would know Mandela's name without scenario planning and the subsequent attention and support those scenarios prompted. Certainly, there have been corporate power plays that encouraged wars—why not a corporate power play that avoided one? Playing out future stories is a good way to blend your goals and objectives with deeply motivating imagined futures.

Finding a Vision story is different from scenario planning in that we aren't testing our goals with lots of different stories but looking for a story that communicates the "desired state" of our goal as a place/time/condition worthy of sacrifice.

Our purpose here is to build a future story that pulls us to it. A "pull" story works best when it conjures positive emotions like desire, hope, belonging, or happiness. Stories based on negative emotions like *fear* (greed is just another word for fear) fuel stress (another word for fear) by feeding perceptions of danger, scarcity, and us/them thinking. Fear is a physiological and psychological state that literally narrows vision and limits creativity. It narrows your peripheral vision to a tiny percentage of the available input and toggles your options back and forth between two options: fight or flight. Fear makes you stupid. It compartmentalizes every

IQ point you have into tiny loops of worst-case scenarios. Hope and love, on the other hand, expand peripheral vision and network to connections and possibilities only obvious to a relaxed eye.

A good Vision story builds resilience and optimism so work groups recover quickly from setbacks and judiciously sacrifice personal gain for group success. It is important to remember that a good Vision story also validates the difficulties of achieving your vision. "Pie in the sky" visions that ignore real pain, sacrifice, and frustration can burn out your optimists and fail to motivate the "realists" in your group. You don't want to lose those people—they are important. You don't want to overpromise either. That's just borrowing trouble.

Vision stories give a lot and they demand a lot. Before we embark on finding a story, you need to do some groundwork to build substance into your story. Begin with your personal vision first. Group Vision stories should be developed from group process.

STEP ONE. What is my vision? Write about a day five or ten years from now that would describe the kind of day you might observe if your dreams came true:

_____

_____

_____

Now list a few of the obstacles that pop up when you imagine this future:

_____

_____

_____

The Vision stories you seek may be found from stories that illustrate your vision or from stories that illustrate overcoming similar obstacles. You will find both as you come up with ideas from the four buckets of stories. Ideally you can find one that blends the *why* and *how* into one. This is a rare gem—a story that not only motivates but suggests strategies to get there.

STEP TWO. Read through these four examples of Vision stories to get your juices flowing with ideas and jot them down as you go along:

A Time You *Shined*

> During the fall of 1992, I was working at J. Walther Thompson in Melbourne, Australia. I had just completed a successful pilot program for the Ford dealer network set to expand in the next year from a budget of $200,000 to $2 million. The powers-that-be decided to bring in someone with more experience to run "my" program. I didn't take it well. Other unpleasant events led me to conclude that I wasn't cut out for advertising. Earlier that year I had attended one of those weekend workshops where I was asked, "If you had all the money in the world, what would you do?" I knew immediately: "I would do something to help groups get clear on who they are and why they are here." I was tired of "unpleasant events" and convinced I could help people avoid turf wars, favoritism, untruths, etc. But that "vision" was so vague so I muddled along without making any real changes.
>
> One night I had a dream that changed everything. I dreamed I was at a train station—a big one with over twenty platforms. I sat with my mother, drinking coffee, surrounded by our luggage waiting for our train, which

was due in an hour or so. I stood up and announced I was going to walk around a bit. I decided to find our platform and check it out. It was a long walk and down an escalator. As I stood on the platform our train arrived—an hour early—and the loudspeaker said it was leaving in three minutes. I didn't have my luggage. I didn't have a ticket. My mother didn't know where I was . . . but I got on anyway. If I took the time to get everything I needed, I would have missed the train. I distinctly remember thinking, "I'll make it up as I go" and began practicing my explanation for the first problem I'd encounter—no ticket to show the guy who checks tickets.

When I woke up that next morning, I knew I would quit my job, move back to the United States, find a graduate program or a mentor, and invent a new career. Some people thought I was having a meltdown—my mother in particular. Common sense says you need to have a job before you quit one—at the very least a general idea of a job. I had neither. On April 23, 1993, I flew home to Louisiana, drove across country that June, and by August I had found both a graduate program and a mentor. By 1997, I had a graduate degree, two years' experience with my mentor, and a contract for my first book. When my book came out, I started my own business. I just got on the train without a ticket or luggage and trusted that I would figure out the details as they arose.

You've done it before and you can do it again. Life spirals around and around again to the same kind of lessons. There is a part of you that wants the same thing today that you wanted ten, twenty years ago. Think back to the last few times you "went for it" and succeeded. Even small wins count. Think of a time when you were in a similar situation facing similar obstacles and you (and your team) made it through.

_____

_____

_____

_____

_____

A Time You *Blew It*

One of my first bosses had to see every letter I wrote and rehearse every presentation I was to make before I was allowed to send or present it to the client. Letters came back from her, dense with red pen marks, deleted sentences, and scribbled rewrites. Presentations were re-arranged and reworded to Linda's satisfaction. I didn't fight her. I had lost all my confidence the year before in a rather brutal public-speaking course, where the in-structor stopped me in the middle of an extemporane-ous speech and the other participants voted me off the stage. I was devastated. *Survivor* may make good TV but it's not a nurturing format for developing communi-cation skills.

My presentations were boring, tedious, and painful for me and for anyone else suffering through them. It was agony. One day I was asked to present a status re-port in Linda's absence. She was off getting her boobs done (you can't make this stuff up). I had no taskmaster to please, so I just did it my way. My fifteen-minute presentation wasn't designed to please Linda but de-signed by me to please the client. And boy did it please the client. I was embarrassed by all the praise I got afterwards. The client congratulated Linda's boss because the only explanation that made sense to them was that my newly coherent and smooth delivery must have been due to his coaching skills. He just smiled.

From that day forward I vowed to never deliver someone else's words or someone else's message. I decided I would be me, do it in my style, take the credit if it succeeded, and pay the price if it didn't. I knew that if I couldn't make the presentation of information or ideas truly mine—then I shouldn't be presenting.

In the same spiral of repeating themes you will find a recurring mistake that sabotages your efforts . . . or used to, anyway. What was it that used to snatch defeat from the jaws of victory? Tell a story about how you used to play this old pattern. Telling the story can help inoculate yourself from repeating this old mistake. When did you give up and regret it? When did you refuse to listen to the quiet voice inside you? When did you have an opportunity to achieve something wonderful but didn't try, gave up, or let someone talk you out of it?

_____

_____

_____

_____

_____

A *Mentor*

If you have ever gotten into trouble for telling the truth then we have something in common. Since I was five years old I've been blabbing uncomfortable truths or naming elephants that might have sat happily unnamed for decades. Rather than an extra dose of courage I suspect my behavior is better described as a total lack of discretion. But since that's who I am, I needed skills. I hunted for someone who could teach me these skills. I need to know how to tell the truth and NOT get burned at the stake. I found a mentor in the man Galileo. He is one of my all time favorite truth-tellers for lots of reasons, but most of all because he did NOT burn at the stake. Others did. One of his contemporaries named Brutus said the exact same things Galileo said and he burned. Galileo was asked by a friend to step in and try to save Brutus. He chose to remain silent. Can you imagine that? Letting someone hang?

This detail forces me to admit there are times when impulse control is the best way to achieve a larger vision. Galileo even signed a confession (even if it does drip with sarcasm), admitting that he was wrong and acknowledging that the sun did in fact orbit the earth. He continued writing and speaking, but he stayed well beneath the radar. His final punishment was that he was confined to his own house in ugly old Florence in his seventies. This was during the Inquisition, when others burned for much worse.

My vision is to tell even dangerous truths, but also to stay alive and keep my clients, and so I regularly ask myself W.W.G. D.? *What would Galileo do?* Any reading of his biography is a lesson on how to be savvy and when to keep my mouth shut. Brutus was someone he knew—an old friend who mouthed off to the extent that he was burned at the stake. Galileo received a letter from a friend begging him to intervene, and yet he didn't. He didn't have enough clout, so he stayed silent.

I'm reminded of the serenity prayer phrase, "the wisdom to know the difference." Galileo had a passion for the truth but he did not have a martyr complex. When strong-armed by the Pope (who might have secretly agreed with his proofs) to sign a confession, he folded like a cheap tent. It was just ink on paper.

But his crowning achievement—still in print—was a story he published where three characters argue the virtues and validity of both sides of the argument. He published his story in a book titled *Dialogue*. Galileo used story to get his points across. His characters make points, ask questions, and expose silliness he was forbidden from discussing. Galileo was a crafty old coot. He was dedicated to the truth *and* he was flexible enough to moderate his approach and silence his ego when danger threatened—lessons I try to remember.

Recognizing a mentor requires humility. Likewise, anyone who inspires humility in you is a perfect prospect to become the focus for one of your Vision stories. Think of any man or woman who inspires you, and set out to tell their story. Research their story without an agenda and you will be blessed with creative insights and perspectives that offer new paths, new strategies, and help you avoid unforeseen obstacles. Every human drama is to some extent a repeat of one that went before. If you look closely you will find a time when an individual you admire faced obstacles similar to yours, overcame those obstacles, and won.

_____

_____

_____

_____

_____

A *Book, Movie, or Current Event*

There are plenty of movies that offer great Vision stories. *Miracle*, about the 1980 U.S. ice hockey team, teaches about cohesion. *Seabiscuit* represents the galvanizing spirit of the underdog. *The Greatest Game Ever Played* straightens my spine as it reminds me that I decide who I am and where I belong—not other people. But all of these movies are about contests—sports where there are winners and losers. I enjoy contests but my overarching vision for my life is not a contest. More than a decade ago I decided to live my life as an artist. I think business and organizations need art as much as any other part of society to express truth, tackle tough subjects, and seek meaning and beauty. I see part of my job as living a creative life so I can bring new thinking to those who don't have time for "white space."

I wasn't sure what changes I'd need to make in order to live life like an artist. I read autobiographical accounts from my favorite artists: Maya Angelou, Johnny Cash, Anne Lamott, C.S. Lewis, and others. I learned that artists aren't slaves to routine. They leave plenty of white space to think and that "thinking" is part of what artists mean when they say, "I'm working." Artists face hopelessness, make mistakes, and invite harsh criticism. I don't like criticism. In order to stay the course, that is the one thing I need the most help with: handling criticism.

Johnny Cash invited lots of criticism, much of it deserved. I was curious, how did he tell the difference between deserved and undeserved criticism? I find it hard to tell the difference when criticism is directed at me.

Johnny Cash was a prolific artist. During his recording career starting in 1955, he released over 450 singles, 1,500 long play albums, and more than 300 compact discs across twenty-six different countries. Each of those sold thousands, some millions. After 1968, when he married June Carter and got his addictions under control, it seems that most fights with his "handlers" were over issues of authenticity. He said in his autobiography, *Cash*, that he got tired of CBS (his record company) telling him about demographics, the "new country fan," the "new market profile," and all the other trends working against him. By 1974, he felt "mentally divorced" from CBS. It all came to a head when Cash gave CBS a record called "Chicken in Black," which was "intentionally atrocious" He even forced CBS to pay for a video shot in NYC where he dressed up like a chicken. The next year (1986) CBS declined to renew his contract. Big surprise. I love this story because it supports my natural inclination to reject numbers that don't create a meaningful connection I can feel in my bones. If it doesn't feel right, I don't do it.

Johnny Cash's long career proves that standing his ground paid off. At age 61 he launched yet another comeback that reached deep into the very demographics CBS would've killed for. Rick Rubin, "in clothes that would've done a wino proud," convinced him that he wanted to produce whatever music Cash wanted to record. Rubin, producer of the Red Hot Chili Peppers and Beastie Boys, told him, "I'm not very familiar with the music you love but I want to hear all of it." Cash asked if he didn't think it might be a stretch to think his music would appeal to a younger audience. Rubin answered that "they only need to see the fire and passion you bring to your music. We'll just be totally honest." Their honesty produced four Grammy-winning albums.

Authenticity—the good and the bad—is synonymous with the Cash legend. Johnny Cash's life is testament to never giving up on your art and to never selling out. When I wear my Johnny Cash T-shirt, strangers

give me the thumbs-up sign in the grocery store. I feel
the same.

Fiction is a dangerous place to go hunting for Vision stories. I
prefer nonfiction for Vision stories because even great fiction is
an invented world designed by one mind—perhaps a genius
writer but not necessarily a genius at living a good life. Fiction
often serves to proselytize, vent, or escape reality. A fiction writer
can bend characters and events in ways that you cannot match
when dealing with reality. It's best to choose nonfiction for Vision
stories. I can see where fiction might work—it is just not something I'm willing to do personally. You may struggle for a story,
but this research (often quite frustrating) forces you to distil your
vision. True stories also reveal obstacles and opportunities you
might not have considered. And once you find one that resonates,
a true Vision story is very powerful. You can also use the movie
or book to prompt dialogue with your work group. This dialogue
can reveal hidden resistance and flesh out incongruent perceptions earlier rather than later. What book or movie inspires you
to do more, be more, last the distance?

_____

_____

_____

_____

_____

_____

STEP THREE. Choose one of these ideas to develop into a story.
Write the story here in your journal. Do not edit. Write in whatever order it comes, including every single detail you can remem-

ber. Provide sensory details for all five senses. Write as much as
you can remember.

_____

_____

_____

_____

_____

_____

_____

_____

_____

_____

_____

_____

_____

_____

_____

_____

_____

_____

_____

_____

_____

_____

_____

_____

_____

_____

_____

STEP FOUR. Now put your journal away and find someone who will listen to a "test-telling" of this story. Tell your story without these notes (storytelling, not story reading!) to someone you trust.

STEP FIVE. Ask your listeners for appreciations. Ask them to respond to your story with any of the following appreciation statements, and record what they say:

"What I like about your story is . . ."

"What your story tells me about you is. . . ."

"The difference hearing your story might make to our working relationship is . . ."

"I can see you using this story when (client situation) in order to (impact) . . ."

_____

_____

_____

STEP SIX. Now write your own thoughts about this story. What do you like best? When you tell it again what do you want to remember to say first or last? Are there any new details you can include to make this story more vibrant or alive? Is there a particular order that is more engaging? Do you need to go back to your story ideas and find another one? Testing up to five ideas for a Vision story is normal. The effort will pay off.

_____

_____

_____

_____

_____

_____

_____

_____

_____

_____

_____

_____

_____

_____

_____

_____

_____

_____

_____

_____

_____

_____

_____

_____

_____

_____

_____

_____

_____

_____

CHAPTER 9

Value-in-Action Stories

ALL STORIES ARE Value-in-Action stories at some level. A simple story about a contractor—who arrived late, did a lousy job, and charged twice his original quote—reinforces the value of cynicism. I've been trying to stop telling it. But it is hard. It is a true story and I'm still ticked off. The question is: Am I still telling this story because I am still ticked off, or am I still ticked off because I am still telling the story? It is impossible to answer that question with any veracity. However, when I balance this story with an equally true story, I feel less cynical.

Derrick, also a contractor, came to my house on a Saturday morning on short notice. He had his young son in tow, on their way to a soccer game, and he took the time to fix a leak in my guest bathroom because my mom was coming to visit on Sunday. He went "above and beyond" the call of duty. Common sense tells me that retelling the second story more than the first leaves me more inspired to go "above and beyond" the call of duty. The first story leaves me feeling rather cynical. Cynicism rarely elicits more than minimum effort.

Stories reinforce the value that is most vibrantly experienced by the listener. Even if your intention is to reinforce the value of reliability, if the primary sensory experience in the story is one of broken promises, it is a victim story. Victim-hood is not a good value to reinforce in yourself or others. Your "I was robbed" stories need to be told and heard so you can process your feelings and move past bad experiences. Telling your story is therapeutic but *not* influential—at least not in the direction you intended. All humans have stories of broken promises, exploitation, and betrayal. The brain is designed to ruminate on these negative experiences to help you avoid repeat performances. Warning stories have their place, but positive Value-in-Action stories will usually require more attention than we naturally would give them. These stories can feel forced—but the payoff is worth the effort.

It takes discipline to consciously tell stories that build values like trust, loyalty, generosity, and excellence into our lives. It also requires a support system. You need someone to listen to your stories of disappointment so you can process those feelings and move past them. Emotions buried alive don't die; they just hijack your communication the next time you run across a good listener or a captive audience.

Stories Frame Experiences

The stories and metaphors used in everyday communication lay the foundation for how we think about the world. Metaphors are mini-stories that help us frame complexity into a familiar package. We use the war metaphor a lot: the war on AIDS, for instance. We use war as a metaphor even though AIDS is a disease—without an emotional agenda, troops, or even a brain. When we channel our desire to find a cure and prevent the spread of AIDS through the metaphor of war it feels more urgent, and for some people more "win-able." Many people like the metaphor of war because it makes them feel stronger to fight a war. War feels more active. Framing the goal as "healing a disease" is gentler and more complex. Metaphors frame and simplify, but sometimes they compartmentalize and oversimplify.

We are often suckered into metaphors that stir our emotions and direct our resources in directions we might not choose if we were paying closer attention. As an example, it is commonly accepted that designing a factory, product, or information system as a "lean mean fighting machine" is a good idea. This metaphor helps you "trim the fat" (metaphor) and "get rid of deadwood" (metaphor). But consider how these metaphors translate when applied to people? People can become "lean mean fighting machines." Perhaps you've dealt with a few of those machine-like people. You might have even felt like a machine yourself. It's a dead feeling. The "lean mean fighting machine" metaphor can dull our humanity and disconnect us from the empathy one flawed human has for another.

Without an equally powerful metaphor for human systems, humans end up acting like lean mean fighting machines in meetings, or treating coworkers like they are "deadwood." Newsflash: That is NOT going to motivate staff or improve communications. Metaphors that improve the design of inanimate things and automated systems can kill the values that preserve human and humane systems.

When a company uses the metaphor "flawless execution" to describe their accounting services—that's good; that is exactly what I want when someone files my taxes: flawless execution. But that company needs complementary metaphors and stories to accommodate the people side—the flawed employees who fall short of perfection. Flawless execution translates into executing the flawed unless tempered with values like trust, tolerance, reciprocity, and forgiveness.

Forgiveness is essential to any sustainable human system. Rules and policies do not accommodate the ambiguities of real life. The customer is NOT always right. One evening—hassled, tired, and angry that my hotel key didn't work—I marched downstairs to the front desk and shoved the card key at the desk clerk saying, "This key doesn't work." I probably even let out a teeth-clenched sigh. The desk clerk grinned ear to ear with a twinkle in his eye, and said, "That might be because this key isn't for our hotel." I looked and sure enough the key I was holding was for the hotel I'd just left. I was wrong and I had been rude, but his mood lifted mine and I grinned back, "Well, then . . . that would be the reason it doesn't work, wouldn't it?" We shared a joke on me.

Mr. "Flawless Execution" could have (and rightly so) embarrassed me for being stupid *and* rude. Instead this man chose to forgive, have some fun, and help me save face in spite of my being quite flawed. Only experience, story, and metaphor can successfully transfer the complex, ambiguous values of humor, tolerance, and compassion.

It's Not Bragging

Your goal is to tell more stories about doing the "right" thing in tough circumstances. Humble people get squeamish because it feels as if they are bragging on themselves. It's not bragging. These stories are an investment in the future of your organization and in the future of the next generation. If you don't tell your stories, your values might die. TV, movies, and MySpace are certainly not focused on transferring values like self-discipline, integrity, or frugality.

The value of integrity-in-action usually occurs without any witnesses. Integrity by definition is doing the right thing when no one would ever know if you cheated, acted selfishly, or fudged a number. If you don't tell your story no one will ever know that you did the right thing, even though it cost you. Besides, integrity means different things to different people. For my father, a retired federal employee and a lieutenant colonel in the Army Reserve, integrity meant that if his boss told him to do something, he did it. To me integrity means if my client asks me to do something that feels wrong—for example, build an image of trust for a company that exploits people—I have to say no.

Values are never clear cut. That's why Value-in-Action stories are vital if you genuinely want to build collective values powerful enough to guide behavior. Incivility has become a problem in many high-tech and high-stress workplaces. Hospitals are both high tech and high stress. Jim Falucci of Veterans Affairs in New York shared a story with his staff recently about how cultural values have shifted around smoking in V.A. hospitals. He remembers a day when people happily smoked inside the hospital. No one explicitly said smoking is okay. It was implicitly okay. However, back then smoking was not allowed on elevators, and Jim was peeved because he seemed to be the only person willing to correct a stranger getting on an elevator with a lit cigarette. "Now" he says, "woe to anyone who dares light up inside the building much less the elevator." His story draws attention to the correlation between speaking up and changing behavior. His point is that in some pockets of the hospital system rudeness is tolerated.

Like smoking was twenty years ago, incivility is implicitly okay. Everyone is stressed out, overworked, and grumpy, and so we tolerate it. As long as people tolerate incivility it continues. It's not as if people aren't doing their job. Staff can follow rules and procedures to the letter and still sound disrespectful, annoyed, or exasperated. Incivility continues when otherwise good people are unaware of their impact on others. It takes courage to be one of the first in your organization to stop tolerating a behavior like smoking . . . or incivility. Values often cost you something in the short term. I have felt a warm conversation chill when I asked a relative to refrain from using racist language. It cost me in the short term but has increased awareness in my family over the long term. Values don't pay off without continuous investments by real people who face real consequences for holding that value.

An organization that professes to value respect should be teeming with stories about respect. If you can't find stories about respect, it doesn't necessarily mean you aren't a good story gatherer. It may mean, instead, that other values are currently more important than respect. I recently worked with a large global company concerned with "hygiene issues"—their metaphor for low trust levels in their market. This company is peerless when it comes to identifying and exploiting market and product opportunities. They truly are one of the best companies in the world in terms of making the right decisions, doing the right things at the right time to make money and to grow market share.

Recently they had so many new products to introduce they called it the "season of swagger." Asked to help them with telling the story of trustworthiness, I called attention to current stories being told by suppliers, customers, and partners. The values of speed, excellence, and growth meant they regularly cut off or ignored those who were slow, flawed, or meticulous. It's a choice. Exploiting every opportunity to grow will not breed trust. Trust is not built from exploitation.

Values Beyond Reason

Like many values, trust is often not technically rational. Trust means I can fall and you won't leave me. Trust means if I sacrifice for your good, you will return the favor in the future. Trust rates good intentions over current results and allows for second chances. Many work groups have tried to use objective reasoning to deal with deep disagreements that provoke strong emotions. It doesn't work.

Objective reasoning is too strict and too dry to inspire or cultivate loyalty from flawed humans. International experience is a good way to decrease blind trust in objective reasoning. When your experience comes from only one culture, certain conclusions seem obvious. An American, for instance, won't notice the arbitrary nature of his understanding of the behaviors he correlates with values like integrity, trust, and success. He might think it is obvious that any good compensation system strongly rewards individual efforts. A Japanese manager might believe just as emphatically that any good compensation system ensures no one individual comes across as more important than the group as a whole. Values create culture and culture creates values. Mix two cultures and you better start by sharing Value-in-Action stories; otherwise you will end up with assumptions that "they aren't trustworthy" or "they don't have integrity," when in truth they simply have a different definition for that value in action.

Mixing cultures breeds conflict that can produce either creativity or distrust. In order to turn conflict into creativity, use Value-in-Action stories to articulate personal values in a way that makes sense and does not feel judgmental to those with a radically different background. Ask an American whether when witnessing a hit-and-run accident he'd turn the driver in, and he won't think twice about an emphatic, "yes." Anyone would, right? Not in some cultures. A Venezuelan witnessing a hit-and-run accident might pretend he didn't see a thing—particularly if that person was his boss. He has a family to feed.

Many heated disagreements can be avoided or at the very least will benefit from sharing Value-in-Action stories. It is an unfortunate consequence of American ethnocentricity that we tend to equate rational thinking with values. Values are designed to guide us when we must make decisions in ambiguous circumstances (i.e., daily life).

STEP ONE. This may be the most important exercise in this book. It is critical to your sense of happiness in the world to know your values and feel that you live up to your own standards. What are your values? It's important to consciously choose your values. Before you look for stories, take some time to think and write down the four most important values that guide your behavior. These change over time, and at any point in your life some will have higher priority than others.

Think about a difficult decision that left you unsure. In the end what did you choose to do? If that action left you feeling like you did the "right" thing, you probably based your decision on a value. If it left you feeling you did the wrong thing, you neglected a value that was part of your internal guidance system.

What are your four core values?

1. _____

2. _____

3. _____

4. _____

STEP TWO. The four buckets are full of Value-in-Action stories. All you have to do is look. Here are some examples to inspire your own story ideas.

A Time You *Shined*

Every January I run a course for people who want to learn how to facilitate dialogue. My second book, *A Safe Place for Dangerous Truths*, lays out a formal process for a very intense type of conversation that peels back hidden agendas and exposes implicit assumptions. I've facilitated this type of dialogue for over a decade, and I can tell you it is not for the weak-hearted. The course is limited to ten participants because everyone brings so much baggage about how people "should" behave in groups and what facilitation "should" be that everyone needs personal attention at some point in the process.

One year I had five people enrolled. It was November and I was probably not going to fill the class. I always run it anyway. The phone rang and the representative of a very large organization asked me how many places I had left. I told him I had five places left. He said, "We'll take all five." Now that might have seemed like good news to most people, but I was thrust into a moral quandary. Each of the five already enrolled participants was self-employed or paying their own way. Each of them worked in different types of industries. If you have ever attended a course where 50 percent of the participants are from the same organization you know that group discussions are dominated by examples from that one organization and their unique issues. I felt it would be unfair to the original five people signed up. They deserved better. Each of them paid out of pocket and the five prospective participants would be attending on their company's dime.

In all good conscience I had to say, "I'm afraid I can't take five people from the same organization. It wouldn't be fair to the rest of the group. I can take two now and we can figure out something in between now and next year or just let them take the course next year." There was a long pause on the other end of the line, "Are you telling me no? You are refusing enrollment?" I tried to explain my reasoning but he would have none of it. "Then we won't be sending anyone." I said, "I'm sorry you feel that way." I was sorry to lose the opportunity, but I still feel like I did the right thing.

You learned your values over time by having those values tested. Each of your core values showed up at some time when you chose that value over an easier alternative. That choice and the circumstances surrounding it are a shining example that will make an excellent Value-in-Action story. There have been many occasions when your values were tested. All you have to do is choose one of these and tell about a time when it would have been easier to do anything but follow the values you listed above—respect, reliability, precision, trustworthiness, compassion, or winning—but you chose the path your core value demanded of you. Tell about all the circumstances and be honest about whether you deliberated over your decision. It makes the story more real to know that you almost didn't do the "right thing."

_____

_____

_____

_____

_____

A Time You *Blew It*

Frankly, I did not expect teaching storytelling at a Navy base would be so enlightening. I was wrong. Our military attracts some of the finest men and women in our country and gives many who would not otherwise begin life with fine qualities, the opportunity to develop them. This is a story within a story, but I'm including both because sometimes stories aren't the same cut into two:

Sixty men and women sat in the training room. The course was open enrollment and, departing from normal military protocol, the participants ranged from very high to low rank, sitting side by side. Both great and small sat together in classroom chairs with built-in desks, just like high school. Storytelling is a great equalizer.

When we broke for lunch, the group swiftly headed to the galley. Except one guy. I hadn't noticed him before. He was small, compact, redheaded, and freckled—one of those people who could be fourteen or forty, it was impossible to tell. We were the last two in the otherwise empty room. I couldn't figure out what he was waiting for. I was waiting for the training manager, Bettye Brumuller, to come get me. She and I were going off base for lunch. She glanced at him as we walked out and said, "End of the month, I just hate that." I look bewildered and she went on, "He's broke—no money for lunch until payday at the end of the week. I see it all the time." I glanced back. He was looking out the window.

We got into her big red Cadillac—Bettye has style—and headed off to get some greens and cornbread. On our way back she gave no explanation as she pulled into the Chick-fil-A drive-thru. She continued chatting in between ordering a sandwich and drink. I assumed someone had asked her to pick something up. When we got back she walked me back to the training room and came inside to set the sandwich and drink on a side table, announcing to the room in general, "Some idiot screwed up our order and gave us an extra sandwich. I didn't want it to go to waste. I figured one of you boys might want it." As I said, Bettye has style.

I left for a minute and when I came back "Red" was slurping down the end of his drink and the bag was wadded up on his desktop. I smiled, called the class to order, and asked who would be willing to share a story next. His hand was up like a shot. I invited him to come to the front, and he told this story:

"I joined the Navy because this girl I liked joined. Of course I never saw her again. (*He paused for the laughter.*) But it didn't matter because for the next fourteen years I was either drunk or stoned most of the time. Two years ago I self-referred myself into a treatment program. It was my own decision. I haven't had any drugs or alcohol for two years. When I sobered up I learned something really important: I HATE the Navy! (*He had to wait a long time for the laughter to die down.*) As a matter of fact, I hate authority in general. But I only have a few more years until I can retire with full benefits. When I retire I'm getting as far away from this life as humanly possible. But, until that day, as long as I'm here I want everyone of you to know you can count on me. I will go where I'm told, when I'm told, and do what I'm told."

The entire room broke into spontaneous applause. A few of the guys slapped him on the back as he returned to his chair.

Owning up to what might otherwise feel shameful is difficult, but it is a ticket to emotional freedom. When you tell a story like this, people deeply appreciate the depth of humility required to admit that you failed your own value system once upon a time. I recommend you look for a story from a chapter in your life that is already closed. You need to be long past feeling shamed by this event. Don't tell it until you have forgiven yourself and have come out the other side. They say tragedy plus time is comedy—wait until you can laugh about it a little before you tell this kind of Value-in-Action story.

Look for stories from the times when you should've done the

right thing but for whatever reason you didn't. There is not a human being alive who doesn't carry these stories. The power of the story lies dormant until you tell it. You will be amazed at how many people will come up to thank you for telling a story about a time when you failed your own standards. It's obvious you aren't condoning failure. What you are doing is demonstrating humility. We all stumble. And some mistakes can never be repaired—but telling the story might help others avoid making the same mistakes.

_____

_____

_____

_____

_____

A *Mentor*

Everyone should have a Value-in-Action story that illustrates what integrity means to them. Once, teaching a roomful of 2,000 retail electronics professionals, I asked them to tell a partner a story of integrity. I was pretty sure they'd come up with stories better suited to their culture than I could. They did. I love this particular story because it is such a "guy" story:

> I come to a lot of these conferences. Most of them like this one (we were in Las Vegas) are surrounded by casinos. I enjoy gambling but I don't enjoy losing. So my buddy Jack and I made a deal where we spread the risk. Whenever we go to a casino together we split our winnings 50/50. It makes it more fun and we have twice the chance to leave a winner.

So last night we were playing black jack and a little roulette, and I was losing. I was tired anyway so I decided to go to bed early—if you call 1:00 A.M. early. Anyway, this morning I'm sitting at breakfast and Jack walks up like a Cheshire cat and slams down $1,500 in cash right next to my coffee cup. I asked him, "What the hell is this?" He says, "We won last night! Three thousand smackeroos and this is your share!" I told him, "Man this is your money, not mine. I whimped out on you last night." He just screwed up his face like I was nuts and says, "A deal is a deal," and walks off. Now that's what I call integrity. He didn't have to share that money with me. I'm not sure that I would've. But I can guarantee that I will in the future—a deal is a deal.

What mentor taught you how to do the "right thing"? Who in your industry, culture, or organization epitomizes the best of the best? If you seek to influence outside your own group you might seek a mentor figure from the culture, history, or ethnicity of your listeners. Don't assume that your mentor will be someone else's mentor when it comes to values. The extra research pays off. When speaking to your own family, organization, or cultural group, all you have to do is find stories of people most admired by this group and you will find Value-in-Action stories. Look to those you admire personally to find examples of your own values in action. It is fun to arbitrarily choose one of your favorite stories about someone you admire and then decode it for the value(s) illustrated in that story.

_____

_____

_____

A *Book, Movie, or Current Event*

Sara Lawrence-Lightfoot's marvelous book, *Respect*, is basically a book of respect-in-action stories.[1] Among those wonderful stories, she tells one about Jennifer Dohrn, who was a nurse-midwife in a clinic in the South Bronx. To me, the most striking detail of Jennifer's story was that Jennifer dressed up for the birth of every baby. When the time was near, she would put on her best jewelry, beautiful clothes, and full make-up, so that "When the baby arrives, his or her first view of life outside of the womb will be lovely."

When I first started speaking I got some negative comments on my evaluation forms about my clothing. They said I was too casual, even "unprofessional." I wasn't dressing like a hussy but more like a frump. These were the days before the cable show "What Not to Wear," or I might have ended up on it. I was under the impression that what I said was more important than how I looked.

This story about Jennifer Dohrn helped me see that my clothing can be viewed as a statement of my respect for others. Over the years I've learned that respect is communicated in a thousand subtle details beyond my extremely reasoned, rational way of thinking. This story in particular communicates how paying attention to symbolic details can communicate to others in a tangible way.

How would a baby know whether Jennifer had applied lipstick or not? She pointed out that the baby's mother would know. The baby's father and siblings would notice. Their behavior would begin to match hers. She's setting an example with lipstick that might result in a more gentle handling, more time cooing, or even an internal commitment to improve the family's standard of living. Just as important: Jennifer knows. She described dressing up for those babies in a way that clearly demonstrated the respect she has for all human life—rich or poor. Like Jennifer, I now pay attention to my clothing and makeup so that anyone can tell at a glance that I'm honored to be hired to train or speak to a group, and that I'm grateful for the opportunity to learn their stories.

Many books and movies are not a showcase for values. If profit and entertainment is the prime motive, I can see why producers might avoid stories that prompt self-examination. Value-in-Action stories often prompt introspection that might leave the listener coming up short. Ideally the story charts a new future of pride in one's values, but the lag time can cut into profits; thus, entertainment will often go light on deep examination of values in action. However, some of these entertainment books and movies intersperse examples of values in action between the car chases and bedroom scenes. Like the Vision stories I think it is important to stay wary of idealized values in action. If a story lacks believability at the theatre or in your reading, you probably can't make it seem believable in a Value-in-Action story.

Sometimes a brief summary of the plot can illustrate a value. Otherwise, choose an old favorite and reread or rewatch it and pause whenever you find a vignette that might turn into a good Value-in-Action story. Keep your journal handy for jotting down ideas. Don't turn your nose up at TV shows— more people might connect to a Value-in-Action story from *The Simpsons* than to a recap of a Dostoyevsky novel.

_____

_____

_____

_____

_____

_____

STEP THREE. Choose one of your ideas to develop into a story. Write the story here in your journal. Do not edit. Write in whatever order it comes, including every single detail you can remember. Provide sensory details for all five senses. Write as much as you can remember.

_____

_____

_____

_____

_____

_____

_____

_____

_____

_____

_____

_____

_____

_____

_____

_____

_____

_____

_____

_____

_____

_____

_____

_____

STEP FOUR. Now put your journal away and find someone who will listen to a "test-telling" of this story. Tell your story without these notes (storytelling, not story reading!) to someone you trust.

STEP FIVE. Ask your listeners for appreciations. Ask them to respond to your story with any of the following appreciation statements, and record what they say:

"What I like about your story is . . .

"What your story tells me about you is . . .

"The difference hearing your story might make to our working relationship is . . ."

"I can see you using this story when (client situation) in order to (impact) . . ."

_____

_____

_____

_____

_____

_____

_____

_____

_____

_____

_____

_____

STEP SIX. Now write your own thoughts about this story. What do you like best? When you tell it again what do you want to remember to say first or last? Are there any new details you can include to make this story more vibrant or alive? Is there a particular order that is more engaging?

_____

_____

_____

_____

_____

_____

_____

_____

_____

_____

_____

_____

_____

_____

_____

_____

_____

_____

STEP SEVEN. In addition to the value I wanted this story to illustrate, what other values are reflected here? What is the strongest sensory experience in this story and what image is most powerful? Is the value I want to express illustrated by the most vibrant parts of my story?

_____

_____

_____

_____

_____

_____

Note

1. Sara Lawrence-Lightfoot, *Respect* (Reading, Mass.: Perseus Books, 1999).

CHAPTER 10

I-Know-What-You-Are-Thinking Stories

PEOPLE NEED TO feel safe. So we make up stories to cast new information about "one more damn thing to do" in a cynical light. We don't come out and say, "I've already decided this is hogwash," but we are often thinking it. It is a delightful surprise for you to mirror someone's secret suspicions in a story without sounding defensive. It is much easier to overcome an objection before it hardens into a position. An I-Know-What-You-Are-Thinking story overcomes objections when they are still soft—merely a "sneaking suspicion." You don't have to read minds. Unspoken objections are easy to anticipate, particularly if you research your audience's point of view.

When a union representative meets with a manager to resolve a grievance, both enter the room with preconceptions and often with defenses up. They are not necessarily aware of their defensive positioning. Rather, they would say they come with an open mind and even genuinely believe their minds are open, but minds don't work that way. Your mind stands guard over your best interests, whether you ask it to stand guard or not. Secret suspicions lurk beneath hearty handshakes and wide smiles. Ms. Manager might secretly think the union guy is full of himself, high on temporary power, or a troublemaker milking a conflict for its drama opportunities. Mr. Union may secretly suspect that Ms. Manager is a ball-busting bitch-on-wheels who has it in for the gal he is representing because of some "woman thing." Either one of them could break the ice and score points by telling a good I-Know-What-You-Are-Thinking story.

Mr. Union might tell about "what my dad taught me about abusing power," or Ms. Manager could relate a story about her first job "when I acted like a bitch and regretted it." Either story could dramatically change the atmosphere. These stories not only overcome unspoken objections without coming off as opposi-tional but may actually validate the objection as reasonable in the first place.

The Power of Validation

Humans hunger for validation. It doesn't cost you a thing, and sometimes you get tangible concessions in return. You can get a discount, free stuff, and more lenient terms in return for the "milk of human kindness." Failing to validate another's point of view can cost you twice the time, money, or effort you might otherwise spend with this person. Anyone who has been to couples therapy surely learned about validation. Even if you think your partner's feelings are ridiculous and not at all what you "meant" her to feel, explaining one more time how she "should" feel makes things worse. When he says to her, "You are being ridiculous," and she says to him, "You are an insensitive clod," both are invalidating the other.

Even if the statements are technically accurate—and often they are—they make things worse. Miraculously, if he would say, "I can see how my little joke about your painting might have felt like a criticism," and she would say, "It makes sense that you would point out that I painted the males with proportions that are anatomically unlikely," they could relax and unlock fixed positions into a less defensive and more open attitude. Validation is the primary dynamic of the I-Know-What-You-Are-Thinking story. This kind of story validates a parked opinion with a "get out of parking free" stamp that frees a former opponent to move away from a parked opinion without feeling like it cost them their dignity.

Many arguments are fueled less by the "need to be right" and more by the chronically unmet need to be heard and respected. Here again, keeping things rational hides the true issues at play. Unhappiness over salary levels, office layout, or the allocation of "good" projects cannot be resolved with objective reasoning because the unhappiness has more to do with the status associated with these prizes than their "objective value." As primates, humans are programmed to be vitally concerned with status. Our brain software is designed to constantly scan the environment for clues as to where we stand in the pecking order. Even random events are interpreted as meaningful.

Anyone who has ever had a bird poop on his head probably found it very hard not to take it personally. Things like that feel personal because we are persons. Pay attention and you will notice most people who advise you to "not take things so personally" are several steps above you in status. Detachment is definitely helpful for leaders. Taking everything personally leaves a leader drained and dysfunctional. However, telling someone else to "not take things so personally" is often a sign that someone is using this advice to ignore hurt feelings.

Teaching leadership in hospital systems gives me an opportunity to see both the good and bad sides of big egos. Surgeons, for instance, need a big ego to slice into someone's flesh. However, a surgeon's big ego can also translate into a lack of respect for others. Many surgeons with big egos find support staff less than supportive (when no one's life is at stake) than they expect. One surgeon I met felt frustrated by failed attempts to train his staff to stop taking his outbursts and snippy retorts personally. Naturally they weren't catching on. Finally, after the training program, he learned to appreciate that his staff took their jobs very personally, as personally as he took his own job. They all consider their roles as vital to patient care. Any comment or action that appeared to disparage their importance felt like a personal attack.

From their point of view, his outbursts and dismissive attitude impaired their ability to do a good job. The penny dropped. He now has an I-Know-What-You-Are-Thinking story ready to tell to anyone who feels ignored when he is in the "nothing and no one else matters" place he goes to in order to be an excellent surgeon. After hearing his story, they see that he can see (validates) how his concentration might appear dismissive, but the truth is that he values their role as much as his own. Now he finds his support staff is much more supportive even when he occasionally crosses a line.

When we urgently want to influence others a most common mistake is to jump right into spin. Wouldn't it be great if we could just tell them what to think and how to interpret a situation? However, if the situation in question felt like an insult, exploitation, or a reduction in status you must first undo the damage done before you offer a new story. The I-Know-What-You-Are-Thinking story is perfect for this purpose. Spin stories sound too much like "love, trust, and fairy dust" and further invalidate current feeling and interpretations of reality. If you don't validate another person's perceptions as legitimate (and I can guarantee they feel legitimate to them) a spin story can leave people feeling insulted, ignored, or both.

When you set out to influence, by definition you set out to change one interpretation of current reality to a new interpretation. Your new interpretation is either not currently popular or actively opposed. Resist the urge to rush to examples and proof for your preferred interpretation of events. It is vital that you first understand and *communicate* your understanding of current interpretations. If you move too quickly, you lose a very important leverage point that could otherwise help you build a sense of common ground.

Telepathic Powers

Another way to earn attention is by displaying your magical ability for mental telepathy. Telling a good I-Know-What-You-Are-Thinking story can seem to your listeners as if you can read their minds and know their secret thoughts. This level of validation and research into their point of view will earn you big points you might need in the future. Luckily, it doesn't take a genius to identify hidden suspicions held by your intended audience. Most of the time, it doesn't even require research. In most circumstances you already know what "secret" objections your listeners hold against your point of view. New ideas naturally activate contrary forces, natural or man-made if only from the inertia of the status quo. These natural psychological forces pull against your new point of view unimpeded as long as they remain undiscussed. But welcome them into the light of day and often they shrivel and disappear in the sunlight of open examination.

> For instance, I've done a surprising (at least to me) amount of work with the intelligence community. One of the issues that secretly matters is my security clearance. In the military, hierarchical status and clearance usually correlate so closely that the two are interpreted interchangeable. If you have high clearance you must be important. If you are important you have high security clearance. I don't have a high security clearance. Therefore I can anticipate that many of my military clients might naturally wonder: How smart or important could she be? Secrecy is a status symbol in the military. It is frequently used to exclude people deemed unimportant

(along with their ideas). In order to earn credibility with highly placed military clients I need to bring the issue into the open and reframe it.

First, I get points simply for knowing that it is an issue. Second, I use those points to create an alternative interpretation for my lack of security clearance. I tell them I have been offered sponsorship through the clearance process several times, and I turned it down. The first time I was told I needed security clearance, I was working with Air Force Intelligence and the "big guy" insisted I join his group for dinner. He told me, "We need to get you security clearance." I told him, "No way." He pulled his chin down and looked at me over his glasses as if I was either dealing drugs or had a body hidden somewhere.

I explained, "You don't want to give me security clearance because I can't be trusted." Okay, I was playing with him a little here but it was too tempting to resist. Before he could launch into me, I continued, "To prepare for this course, I made a big yellow file that says 'Air Force Intelligence.' Last week I had a pedicure so I took the big yellow file to read at the salon. I finished my pedicure, walked out, and left the big yellow file in the salon—sitting right on top of the other reading material, a big yellow file with a label that said: Air Force Intelligence."

I do that sort of thing all the time. I am absent minded. I did not inherit the genetic code for secret keeping. I sometimes think that I wrote the book, *A Safe Place for Dangerous Truths,* simply to decrease the number of secrets other people expect me to keep. However, I strongly believe it is one of the main reasons I'm good at what I do. I make tools and design methods to decrease the amount of unnecessary secrecy clogging your lines of communication. By revealing unnecessary secrecy I can help your group improve communication and save time. But for goodness sake don't tell me anything that needs to remain secret, or anything that could send me to jail. My value to you is much higher without security clearance.

This story names a hidden assumption often invisible even to those who hold the assumption. It examines the hidden association between "smart/important" and "security clearance." I create the possibility of a new interpretation by introducing the possibility that I was offered security clearance (it is very expensive) and I turned it down for good reasons. It destabilizes the hidden assumption long enough for me to make a case that the two aren't always interchangeable. If I don't do it up front, I may lose my opportunity. In most military situations, what they need to discuss feels dangerous because it involves important egos and challenges common practice, not because it threatens national security. Thus this story also serves another "I know what you are thinking" purpose by preempting the "I can't discuss that" dodge hiding behind the guise of protecting national security, when in fact it is a ruse to avoid discussing uncomfortable issues.

Framing

Influence is much easier if you can control the sequence of information that best supports your point of view. For instance, the "after" pictures that advertise a diet wouldn't sell many diet plans without the "before" pictures. For a comprehensive review of the magic of sequence and frame on perceptions I highly recommend, *Influence: Science and Practice,* by Robert Cialdini.[1] One of my favorite examples from his book cites a letter from a college freshman to her parents. In the beginning of her letter she tells her parents that her skull fracture is healing, the fire wasn't so bad after the janitor offered to let her stay with him, and oh, by the way, they are expecting a baby together. Her last paragraph reveals that there was no skull fracture, no fire, no janitor, and no pregnancy, *but* she did get a "D" in chemistry and just wanted to put the bad grade into the proper perspective.

Perspective can make a $100 donation seem huge (feed a family for a year) or tiny (one month of mocha lattes) in the same letter. Fundraisers have learned they can improve perceptions of a target donation amount by listing it as a second option, dwarfed by the first option they rarely expect to receive. Saying "no" to a first request leaves a donor with a lingering sense of obligation that increases the likelihood of a "yes" to the second request. Children learn this trick early. The question "Mommy, can Billy and I ride our bikes to the gun show?" gets a quick "no" that makes the next question "Then can Billy come over to play?" seem like a bargain.

Stories allow you to condense a series of interactions into a simulated experience that feels interactive to your intended audience. When they imagine themselves as one of the characters, they personally experience the story. You can walk a listener through an experience that properly frames your next point. Common experiences are good sources for stories that pull the listener into the experience. For instance, adolescence dealt most of us a series of humiliations that prove in some ways we are all the same. A story that prompts listeners to reexperience adolescent humiliation builds a bond that can weaken divisiveness on the next point. The "Blew It" story in the following examples illustrates one way to do this.

STEP ONE. The magic of I-Know-What-You-Are-Thinking stories is like any magic—it requires a lot of preparation, a deeper understanding of how human attention operates naturally, and practice. Validation and contrast framing are only a couple of applications you will discover when you begin experimenting with these kinds of stories. Choose one individual or one group and itemize the objections they have to your new ideas or methods. It might help to pretend to be this person or someone in the group and complete the sentence: "What I hate about that idea is. . . .":

_____

_____

_____

_____

_____

STEP TWO. Once again we look to our four buckets for examples of I-Know-What-You-Are-Thinking stories. Jot down your own ideas after each of the examples.

A Time You *Shined*

As a facilitator, I am often lumped in with the collective bad experiences a group may have had with "facilitator types." We've all had bad experiences. Even smart, optimistic groups are wary of some stranger who proposes to lead (control) their process and agenda for two days. Sometimes I start by telling this story.

> My favorite introduction by a client to a group happened in Aspen. A group of very smart, very successful executives gathered to work and play for a weekend. The woman who introduced me said, "This is Annette. I promise you, she doesn't use chimes." They applauded. I knew there was a story there. They told me that a past president had hired one of those "woo-woo" facilitators in long flowing clothes who used chimes to

indicate the end of breaks. I suspect she was not very good at her job. The group must have been slow to come back after breaks, and I imagine the chime lady became more rigorous with her chimes. Whatever happened, she really got under their skin. So, during the next break someone kidnapped her chimes and left a ransom note. The best part of the retreat for them were the series of ransom notes and the increasingly less "woo-woo" reactions of the chime lady.

I do not even own chimes—except for the ones on my porch, and they were gifts. When I facilitate a group, I'm all about progress, resolution, and action. Yes, I may ask you to admit that you have emotions at some point. If those emotions are counterproductive to the group's goals we may actually have to discuss those emotions at a level that feels personal. However, I promise . . . no chimes.

This type of story translates "shined" into "a time I felt the exact same way you feel now." If your intended audience is suspicious then tell a story of a time when you were *justifiably* (never belittle another person's caution) suspicious, decided to trust, and were glad you made that decision. Think about your intended audience and imagine all the forces pulling them in the opposite direction of how you'd like them to think. Use rich description and respect as you try to think of a time when you had the same kind of forces pulling you.

_____

_____

_____

_____

_____

A Time You *Blew It*

I try to avoid using the word "leadership." Given the opportunity I usually point out that I think the word should be spelled with a "t" instead of a "p" for all the good most "leadershi***" theories and books deliver. But I must admit that groups need leader types, and some behaviors work better than others. I also think that gender makes a difference. I'm not altogether sure what difference it makes, but when a woman acts like a man she usually pays a price—even if I can't define to my own satisfaction what the hell I mean by "acting like a man."

Teaching women how to be better leaders is a perfect place for "I know what you are thinking" stories. One of my recent experiences was with a group of international (less than 10 percent American) women in Europe. I began by telling this story:

> When I was in elementary school I loved to feel special. I liked to be left in charge of anything because it made me feel special and because I was naturally bossy. In sixth grade I was given a little sheriff's badge and was told to watch the first graders during recess on rainy days so the first-grade teacher could get a break. To entertain them (or me) I taught them how to march in formation with band music (I'm not making this up) and I rewarded those who participated with peppermint candies. I was a little monster. It was my first experiment in leadership, and I learned that peppermint candies or not, some kids simply did not participate because they didn't want to. I also learned that nice kids slipped the nonparticipating kids candies and my reward system was immediately diffused with lack of compliance. Hmmm . . . I learned that you can't mandate cooperation.
>
> In junior high I noticed that the popular girls got all

the cooperation they wanted. Geek that I am, I decided to study the elements and behaviors of popularity so I too could be popular. In the midst of my research a new girl joined our class and asked me who was popular. I decided to help her out and wrote a two-page note on lined notebook paper that not only named the hierarchy of popularity at Lakeshore Junior High but added useful tidbits of information, such as what to wear and where to buy the appropriate plaid baggie pants that were popular in 1973. This young lady promptly used my letter, though not in the way I intended. She took it straight to the popular girls cited and earned her place among them by offering my humiliation as proof of her eligibility. That pretty much put an end to my scientific approach to popularity.

By high school and college I learned that while I could not be popular, I could be useful. Being useful by doing all the work earned me a certain level of leadership potential because I became visible to the kids who cared about a certain club or the junior/senior prom decorations. My new strategy was to trade work for attention. I still use that strategy more than I should, and I'm guessing there are a lot of women who do. Women often make ourselves indispensable to earn a place at the table.

By the time I hit the working world I had tried lots of strategies. It wasn't until I studied group process that I realized that groups have patterns, and if you can predict the patterns of the group you can be in the right place at the right time. That sort of knowledge is power. I also learned about how ruthless groups can be to members who are innovative (deviant) or perceived as weak. Different behaviors will be interpreted differently depending on the stage of the group's development. That's what we are here to learn. No matter what strategies you currently use, this one will only add value and save time.

This could be a story of how you allowed your personal objection to an idea cheat you of an opportunity. Perhaps you can tell (like the story above) about traveling different paths of interpretation and found each a dead end. If you convincingly take them on a tour of genuine experimentation with valid-sounding ideas you can actually leave people feeling satisfied that they have explored a particular path of thinking with due diligence and can now move on to another interpretation. Consider the past experiences causing this group or this individual to resist your point of view. Plot the series of experiences that might cause them to interpret your point of view as dangerous, foolish, or simply not worth it. Demonstrate how deeply you understand their objections by telling a story that validates them.

_____

_____

_____

_____

_____

A *Mentor*

Teaching USAID staff to tell stories has been one of my favorite jobs over the last decade. The men and women of USAID might single-handedly earn back much of the love and appreciation the United States has lost, if only the world could hear their stories. These are some of the smartest, most dedicated people I've ever had the privilege to know. Most speak several languages,

have lived in many cultures, and hold Ph.D.s in an array of com-
plicated subjects. However, the story I want to tell you here is a
mixed bag I use specifically with USAID people, because they
can be very hard on themselves. There are times when smart high
achievers can only become better leaders after they learn to forgive
themselves for their mistakes.

One of the most articulate, beautiful women I've met in a long
time was in a USAID group. Delia (name changed) must have
inherited the carriage and dignity of the African queens she was
surely descended from. Growing up in a ghetto of Detroit did not
bend her. After getting advanced degrees and joining the Foreign
Service, she spent much of her time in Africa. Her last post had
been in Nigeria where this story occurred.

She started by saying:

> I sent my eight-year-old daughter to a local public
> school in Nigeria. So when I was asked to serve on the
> school board I happily accepted. However, the board
> wanted me to chair. I declined, saying that the chair
> should be a Nigerian rather than a foreigner. I actively
> lobbied for a particular Nigerian woman who had a
> Ph.D. in education and who was very visible in the
> community. Sure, I heard a few warnings about this
> woman's character, but I felt the issue of citizenship was
> more important.

She paused for a really long time and foreshadowed the rest of
the story by saying, "She really did seem qualified."

> Once we started having meetings I saw the problem.
> This woman was arrogant, opinionated, rude, and con-
> trolling. She had no idea how to run a meeting. They
> went too long and even after they were over, every board
> member would call me up that night to complain and

ask me to do something. It was taking over my life, so I finally agreed. I had done my best to coach *them* to do something, but she ran over them like a freight train. I told them I'd speak to her at the next meeting as long as they would back me up.

At that next meeting this woman started doing what she always did. She cut people off. She railroaded her agenda items. So I asked if I could make a comment on the process. She turned to me and to this day I have no idea what happened. All I know is that I lost it. I lit into that woman like hell's fury. I called her names. I called her every name except child of God. I have no idea how long it lasted but my eyes started to refocus and I suddenly saw myself surrounded by wide eyes and dropped jaws. I said, "I think I should leave now" and got myself the hell out of there.

I got home, sat down, and thought, "What have I done?" I was horrified. Within the hour I realized what I had to do. I started at the top of the list and called each and every member and apologized. The next day I went in person and apologized to her. She was less than gracious but I kept my dignity.

When I tell about Delia I'm talking about me, too. I get passionate about issues, and sometimes I can be short with people. I also have a temper. If I could have had it surgically removed I would have. It seems to be here to stay, so I try to apologize in advance. I can't guarantee that I won't "lose it" at some point as a long-term member of a working group. But I can guarantee that I will correct myself quickly and apologize.

You may find an analogy of your circumstances either in your own past, a historical event, or preferably in the history of your target audience. Do some research to see if you can find whether the current problem isn't a repeat of a pattern of problems for this particular culture or work group. If it is a repeating loop, tell the story again to give them an opportunity to do things differently this time. Start from the point of view of your target audience. Research the individuals who they feel illustrate their values, and see if you can tell a story that shows you too revere these persons as good examples.

_____

_____

_____

_____

_____

A *Book, Movie,* or *Current Event*

Anyone who has served on a neighborhood committee has experienced the full range of insanity simple issues can invoke in otherwise sane people. In my neighborhood the insanity erupted over a motion to redistrict our 1920s neighborhood as a historical district. My neighborhood is modest and diverse. Many professors from the local university live here, and some front yards sport bizarre sculptures. Two families consider "Christmas lights" a year-round opportunity to express themselves, and several neighbors are conjuring sustainable eco-systems instead of grass in their yards. We may not like the paint color our neighbors choose—but we will die defending their right to paint their house purple if they want. (Initially a sign of protest, one house is still purple with pink and purple columns.)

The young lawyer who is president of our local neighborhood association is a newcomer. His efforts were central in pushing the redistricting effort I now refer to as the "hysterical district" era. The ensuing conflict pitted neighbor against neighbor. Long meetings, angry letters with fifteen signatures, and plots to undermine the "other side" replaced pot-luck pumpkin-carving parties. I was targeted by the board as breaking the rules. I asked for a spot on the agenda of the next board meeting and began with this I-Know-What-You-Are-Thinking story:

We are North Carolinians so I suspect all of us here have seen at least one or two episodes of the *Andy Griffith Show*. The divisiveness in our neighborhood recently reminds me of one particular episode from that series. Do you remember the one when Barney was cleaning out files and ran across a case that had never been closed? The case accused Floyd the barber of assault. It is hard to imagine Floyd raising his voice, much less assaulting anyone. Barney insisted that he would "get to the bottom of this" and marched down to the barbershop.

One interview led to another. Barney reported that Floyd had punched Charlie Foley in the face. Neither of them could remember why, *until* Barney's dogged questions reignited the old conflict and the angry emotions. Andy tried to convince Barney to let it go, but the damage was done. That afternoon Floyd came in with a new black eye, followed by a long line of Mayberry's citizens also sporting black eyes, all with new assault charges to file. It's a typical Barney chaos episode, but it resembles our neighborhood lately. I appreciate that each of you is dedicated to your position and to our neighborhood. But I'd like you to reflect on the recent enthusiasm with which you have been enforcing rules and pursuing legal action. I appreciate the enthusiasm you have put into your efforts to make this a good neighborhood. But I think goodwill is as important as property values, and lately it feels that despite your good intentions this group is perceived by some of us in the neighborhood as operating like a Barney Fife. I would like us to think of how we can be more like Andy and less like Barney.

The Barney in the room simply squinted in confusion and started to prattle the minute I stopped talking. But the others—my true target audiences, who are naturally inclined to calm disputes like Andy rather than stir them up—could see our local Barney Fife had gone too far. I'd like to think this story validated their inclination to override strict legalities and curb Barney's enthusiasm. Within the year, Barney was no longer president and we now have a more mellow, wise "Andy" in his place. We might even have a pumpkin-carving party this October.

Use a scene from a book, movie, or current event to illustrate solidarity, make connections, or diffuse objections. There are plenty of examples. Note a good scene when you see it, because these aren't usually the scenes that will stick in your memory. By the time you need it, even if you can remember the title of that book or film, you are not likely to remember the scene with enough detail to tell it. Notice the scenes that shift the meaning of an event by changing the frame. Choose a scene that overstates your case, so that you can make fun of it (for example, a liberal making fun of Michael Moore). Use a classic clip that illustrates a concept currently held but give it a new interpretation.

STEP THREE. Choose one of these ideas to develop into a story. Write the story here in your journal. Do not edit. Write in whatever order it comes, including every single detail you can remember. Provide sensory details for all five senses. Write as much as you can remember.

STEP FOUR. Now put your journal away and find someone who will listen to a "test-telling" of this story. Tell your story without these notes (storytelling, not story reading!) to someone you trust.

STEP FIVE. Ask the listeners for appreciations. Ask them to respond to your story with any of the following appreciation statements, and record what they say:

"What I like about your story is . . .

"What your story tells me about you is. . . .

"The difference hearing your story might make to our working relationship is . . ."

"I can see you using this story when (client situation) in order to (impact) . . ."

_____

_____

_____

_____

_____

_____

_____

_____

_____

_____

STEP SIX. Now write your own thoughts about this story. What do you like best? When you tell it again what do you want to remember to say first or last? Are there any new details you can include to make this story more vibrant or alive? Is there a particular order that is more engaging?

_____

_____

_____

_____

_____

_____

_____

_____

_____

_____

_____

_____

_____

Note

1. Robert Cialdini, *Influence: Science and Practice* (Needham Heights, Mass.: Allyn & Bacon, 2001).

PART THREE

Perfecting the Craft

CHAPTER 11

Experience Is Sensory

HUMANS EXPERIENCE THE world through five primary channels: what we smell, taste, hear, touch, and see. Perceptions that begin as raw data coming in by way of our senses are then matched to an existing pattern. Because any one "thing"—apples, for instance—displays wide ranges of size, color, and shapes, the brain is designed to accept a "close enough" match rather than seeking a literal exact replica. When we look into a pasture, our brain initially registers the colors brown and white, low sustained vocalizations, and barnyard smells. In the split seconds required to comprehend that sensory data, your brain has found and chosen the perception known as "cow." Objectively, the vast array of patterns that fit the sensory pattern we call cow are not the same at all. Subjectively, we only pay attention to the similarities. We know a cow when we see one. We are sure of that "fact."

If you have ever made fun of your sixth-grade teacher by calling her a cow, you used the power of associations inherent in perception. You probably discovered that you could enhance the vibrancy of the perception of teacher as cow by making mooing noises and by mimicking the rotary chewing motion of a cow chewing cud. You were a little genius storyteller—and still are, when you get back to the basics. Too many courses on psycho-graphics, demographics, and market segmentation have eroded your connection to the physical origins of storytelling.

Analysis and high-level conceptualization are very important tools, but once you know your target's statistics, these abstractions of reality are too hypothetical to stimulate sensory experiences that originate perceptions and emotions. Sure, a lone number can take you on a roller coaster of emotions (for example, stock prices) but only because of the physical associations you have with high versus low numbers: Mercedes versus a used Ford, champagne versus beer, retirement on a golf course versus a job as a security guard at the mall. It is what the number means in terms of the well-being of your body, spirit, and environment that stimulates emotions.

Storytelling intentionally uses sensory language or sensory experiences (Disneyland, Canyon Ranch Spa, etc.) to stimulate desired patterns of association and create new patterns of association:

Roller Coaster = Fun; Disney = Roller Coaster; therefore,
Fun = Disney

The simultaneous stimulation creates new associations.

When you activate memories of a cow (chew, moo, blank stare) and associate those patterns with some poor teacher, you are using a basic building block of storytelling. Never mind that there is no plot. Unless you are studying storytelling for literary purposes, the "requirements" of plot and character can be more intimidating than helpful. Ground yourself in the basics of sensory stimulation, and the rest will follow.

New patterns are built from existing patterns. For instance, if someone has never been to Russia, I can take them there with a story, but I have to use known sensory experiences as building blocks to develop the scenery, characters, events, and consequences. Most people already know what snow is. They have also seen old ladies that are poor. They have seen homeless people in big cities. I can use those building blocks to tell a story about seeing a Russian woman who appeared homeless. The bias in my selection of sensations to stimulate can't be overstated. All storytelling is inherently subjective.

While I was in St. Petersburg, Russia, I was told that older women were a large segment of the homeless population. I saw old women with tattered dresses and coats, selling small trinkets and handkerchiefs rather than begging for rubles. You might begin to picture this scene using the sensory-building details your brain rushes to provide. If you have seen *Dr. Zhivago* you might use the train scene for background. Then my telling of this story begins to frame your conclusions about this scene:

> In Russia, many old women have no safety net because the shift to a free market from communism was abrupt and left millions of people who were subsidized all their lives without enough time to build up savings or assets.

Anchor this with more sensory data:

> The woman burned into my memory stands in the freezing rain with as much dignity as she can, wearing an old crocheted sweater under her coat. The sweater was too fine to be warm and had one rhinestone button left. Her eyes were harder than I expected, when I bought one of her handkerchiefs.

Now the real spin starts. Once I've created a mental image with added sensory details, I can direct the emotions her image generates in you to several equally viable "stories" that call your own future into question and create new associations for the emotions her image may stir up in you (anxiety, despair, pity, discomfort).

A Democrat from the United States might continue by saying social security is vital to a free market economy because otherwise people fall through the cracks. A Republican might emphasize how years of government subsidies became so large they collapse under the burden and leave people trained to rely upon the state, with no skills or savings to support themselves in their old age. Every story is spin, depending on how you tell it. Shouting your own conclusions, like "Social Security is BAD" or "Social Security is GOOD," neglects to anchor your desired associations with the physical experiences; emotions lay the foundation for new associations.

Climb back down the mental ladder of conclusions you may have reached years ago, all the way to the sensory experiences that were your original raw data. Revisiting these original events helps you create a story with similar sensory experiences that will create similar perceptions for your listeners. When your listeners take in these sensory experiences in the desired order, you take them rung by rung through the steps of discovery and conclusions up the ladder you wish them to climb.

Regardless of what conclusions a story reinforces, it all begins with powerful sensory memories that activate strong good or bad associations, so you can direct those emotions toward new associations. When the new associations are stimulating enough to be remembered or retold, every "reexperiencing" of the new associations further anchors the patterns and increases the probability that future events will trigger your new patterns of association. This is how urban legends gain acceptance—not because of their factual bases—but because of their power to stimulate strong emotional reactions.

Urban legends thrive when they trigger retelling urges inspired by strong emotional associations (e.g., Warning! Warning!). Vibrancy imprints imagined sensory memories before doubt has a chance to slam the door shut. The first time most people hear or read the "stolen kidney" legend about waking up in Las Vegas in a bathtub of ice without their kidneys, they imagine the ice in the bathtub, picture the hotel bathroom, and see the handwriting on the note that tells them to call the hospital—all before their frontal lobes have a chance to challenge the plausibility of strangers harvesting kidneys by drugging hotel guests.

Sure-Fire Sensory Associations

Urban legends display an array of sure-fire associations, mostly useless because they are total fabrications, but educational nonetheless. What do these "stories" have in common? *NASA Experiments with Sex in Space; Nostradamus Predicted 9/11 Attack; Spiders Under the Toilet Seat; Bill Gates to Share His Fortune;* and the worst: *Young Cancer Victim Needs Your Help.* All of them activate enough emotions to momentarily override rational reasoning.

The "Spiders under the Toilet Seat" story is particularly interesting. It is a good example of a story that generates a physiological response. The author of this hoax used sensory details that are so vivid they feel true. The first bites "happened" at an Olive Garden restaurant (specific—a place you know, even if you haven't been there) from a two-striped Telamonia (*Telamonia dimidiate*) spider (such a scientific sounding name creates validity). A realistic sounding history provides a plausible back story: A lawyer from Jacksonville returned from Indonesia (familiar sensory details: lawyer, Jacksonville, Indonesia) and ultimately died from a puncture wound on his right buttock. Your brain connects the dots: Hey, that spider must have hidden in the lawyer's suitcase from Indonesia. I'm guessing very few people can read the original e-mail without clinching their right buttock muscle away from an imaginary spider bite. Once a story stimulates a physical sensation in your listener's body and is associated with highly familiar or strongly emotional experiences, it has sticking power.

Most people could use a lesson in sensory stimulation. One of my heroes already understands the power of stories to bring numbers to life. Economist Steven Levitt's book, *Freakonomics,*[1] is full of stories that use emotionally charged associations (e.g., "Why do crack dealers live with their mothers?" and "How are real estate agents like the KKK?") to frame his numbers with imagined consequences.

He is a master at stimulating sensory and emotional sensations that correlate with the questions he asks and the answers he finds. I heard him speak at a building industry conference. If possible, he is even a better storyteller in person than in his books. He began with what I might call an I-Know-What-You-Are-Thinking story. This story demonstrates a reliably vibrant sensory hook: the fart. Notice how he anchors his story with familiar and specific details:

> A recent survey of economists asks "what is the most important skill for an economist?" Seventy percent answered "a proficiency in math," and only 2 percent answered "a good working knowledge of the economy." [*Pause for laughter.*]
>
> I am *not* good at math. I recently went to my high school reunion and my math teacher, Mr. Drexel, remembered my name. He said "Aren't you the one who got 2 out of 5 in calculus?" I had to answer "yes." Apparently I got the lowest score of any of his students . . . ever. That's why he remembered me. My first math class at MIT, I turned to a classmate and asked, "Hey, is there a difference between the curly d and the straight d?" The guy just looked at me with pity and said, "You are in SO much trouble."
>
> I was so far behind my peers there was no way I

could catch up. I wondered what to do and then I remembered a story my father told me. When he was in
medical school, his mentor took him aside. Apparently
his aptitude wasn't so stunning either. His mentor told
him, "Levitt, you don't have much talent for medical
research. There are two ways you can go here. You could
fight your way among the crowds of people who choose
the most popular areas to research, or you can find an
area where NO ONE is researching and own it." That
is how my father decided to specialize in intestinal gas.
In fact, he eventually became known as the "King of
Farts." I took his words to heart and looked for my
niche. *Freakonomics* is to traditional economics what intestinal gas is to traditional medicine.

Levitt starts with a sensory memory most of us share: high
school math. Listeners' memories flash a scene from their high
school math class: guaranteed common experience in that crowd.
My math teacher was Mr. Jackson. (Yours?) Levitt's story is en-
dearing and preempts the audiences' expectations for him to display math genius behaviors. He establishes his own anti-math
genre of economics as, if not superior, certainly more fun than
the egghead version. Describing his dad as the "King of Farts"
brilliantly calls out our inner kid, who is always willing to snicker
at a fart reference. With this simple story Levitt connected to the
audience, made his point, and guided expectations to match what
he planned to deliver. It's much easier to satisfy expectations
when you set them up to match what you intend to offer.

Levitt interacts with people as much, or more than, with numbers. It is an active participant in real life. His curious explorations
of the real lives of others supply him with stories that pop readily
to mind whenever he needs to explain a concept. Those who
never venture into the world don't have many stories to tell.

Full Body Research

Simply identifying the age range and habits of your target audience is not enough. Objective data describes from the outside in. Storytelling starts from the inside out. This means you shut off your computer, set aside the marketing research (after you've read it) and get out there and interact personally with the people you wish to influence. If you want to ignite your creative intelligence, give your body and senses something to work with. Your brain may process abstract data, but only your body can take in the sights, sounds, smells, tastes, and feelings that stimulate creative approaches at the sensory level. Statistics and reports don't stimulate your senses to identify sensory connections that might attract your target's attention long enough to establish a new association or new story.

Use your experiences to connect to your audience's experiences. Find common ground and use it as a bridge for connection. Don't send other people to research the market—go out there yourself and educate your body as well as your brain. The ideas you reap from full body research equip you with stories that stimulate creativity. A recent article in the *New York Times* by William C. Taylor profiled the kind of research that finds stories.[2] The hedge fund, Second Curve Capital (focused on bank and financial services stocks) regularly sends its employees—the analysts, compliance officer, computer geeks, and receptionists—to the streets to do full body research. For this "branch hunt" they are equipped with digital cameras, audio equipment, and crisp $100 bills to capture "flesh and blood experiences" of being a customer. Brown's favorite story is about trying to open an account at a Chase bank and mentioning that he was switching from Citibank. The Chase employee said, "I'm surprised you want to switch, I have my account at Citibank."

Brown says, "The biggest mistake companies make is managing to the averages. How long, on average, to open an account?

What's the average level of customer satisfaction? Averages hide as much as they reveal." Like we discover through the art of storytelling, much of reality is hidden by averages and numbers. Only full body research that results in "flesh and blood experiences" (a/k/a stories) reveals real-life experiences that tell the "rest of the story" that numbers leave out. Any situation you seek to understand for purposes of influence or to gauge future actions is best researched personally with as little an agenda as possible.

In Nigeria I had the opportunity to look for "stories" that women tell themselves about power. I told a story first—an English folktale called "Lady Ragnell"—and asked the women present to tell me a story in return about the last time they felt powerful. One woman told of having enough of her own money to lend a nephew $200 without asking permission from her husband. Another told of demanding an arrogant doctor recheck the leg of a neighbor's child to make sure he hadn't left some glass in his leg (he had). And a Muslim woman told of asking an administrator who denied receiving a timely application from a student to look at her face, against Muslim custom, and check again on his assertion that "he had never seen her." He had been holding the student's application back waiting for a bribe. She knew he was lying. She called him on it. Numbers from a survey analysis of women in Nigeria would not—could not—tell me what these personal experiences reveal.

Anyone who can't think of a story about their company culture or customers is spending too much time in their office looking at numbers and not enough time with the real people who live in the world he or she wants to influence. Empirical research leads to bad ideas, like brochure campaigns about diabetes in poor communities. Money is wasted because those brochures hit trash cans by the thousands. Spending a week in your targeted community without a survey to hide behind is likely to reveal flaws in thinking, such as: distributing brochures = better education about diabetes. These brochures are never read and don't do a damn thing to improve eating habits in the obese. If all medical researchers who perform studies lived with their "population" for a week or more, we would see new kinds of research (not to mention a heightened appreciation for those who research intestinal gas).

Better still, wouldn't it be nice if all the gatekeepers at medical journals (ad agencies, marketing departments, and product design groups) got the same opportunity? Criteria that are easy to research and most pure in a scientific sense are not necessarily the most useful in changing behavior. When subjective issues are prevented from "distorting" research, the results are stripped clean of context. It may be accurate, but isn't emotionally stirring and often leads to ineffective "solutions."

The risk of course is that full body research will deconstruct cherished assumptions, reveal flawed logic, and topple ivory towers. Yes, storytelling can take us backwards before we get to go forwards again. Chapter 12 discusses the potential for turf wars that might erupt when discoveries reveal a bit more reality than some people find comfortable.

In the meantime, practice recreating flesh-and-blood sensations in your stories by using ones that are familiar. Experiment with the following exercise by creating sensations in your own body. If a story doesn't work on you, it probably won't work on others. Practicing creating sensations will deepen your understanding and raise your standards. Our purpose is to elicit sensations that make your story feel like a real-life experience. Here is a little example:

> Imagine a cutting board, and on that board a juicy lemon warm from sitting in a sunny window. You can smell the oils of the zest. Imagine a very sharp knife and pick that knife up and cut the lemon in half. See the two halves rock away and beads of lemon juice collect and then drip down into a puddle. Now you can smell

the juice as well as the zest. Take one of the halves and cut it in half again. Pick up one of the quarters and bring it to your mouth and bite deep, wrap your lips around it to make a yellow smile (like when we were kids), and let the juices run down your chin.

What happened? Did you feel your saliva glands tingle, did your mouth water? That's because your imagination thought there really was a lemon. This is how story works. It activates the power of the imagination to simulate a real experience.

Your goal is to tell a story that activates the imagination of your listeners so they see, hear, smell, touch, and taste (through imagination) your story as if it were really happening. That is vibrancy. Done well, the experience records in the brain as deeply as a real-life experience.

Practice

Choose one of your story ideas and develop vivid, stimulating descriptions for each of the five senses that build context for your story. Don't cheat and hop around to different stories—you won't learn as much that way. This is not a list of things you necessarily will tell; most simply make your story more real in your own mind. These details help you viscerally reexperience the story. When your imagination is so vividly stimulated with the "reality" of the story, other people begin to feel that reality too.

Don't worry about whether you will actually use the details— that's not the point. This is practice to help your brain develop good habits in physically reexperiencing the story yourself as you tell it so the "magic" happens in your tone, facial gestures, body movements, timing, and word choice. Tone, gestures, timing, etc. flow effortlessly when your mind is reexperiencing the sights, sounds, taste, smells, and tactile sensations of your story.

Story: _____

(_Brainstorm as many details as you can for this story. Don't worry about order._)

Taste

_____

_____

_____

Touch

_____

_____

_____

Smell

_____

_____

_____

Sounds

_____

_____

_____

Sights

_____

_____

_____

Now tell the story (without your notes) to a low-risk listener and see how it goes. Record your experience:

_____

_____

_____

_____

_____

_____

_____

_____

_____

_____

_____

_____

_____

_____

Notes

1. Steven Levitt and Stephen Dubner, *Freakonomics: A Rogue Economist Explores the Hidden Side of Everything* (New York: HarperCollins, 2005).
2. William C. Taylor, "Get Out of That Rut and Into the Shower," *New York Times*, August 13, 2006.

CHAPTER 12

The Gift of Brevity

A S MUCH AS I'd like this chapter to be brief, brevity demands an enormous investment of time and energy. As Goethe put it in a letter to a friend, "If I had had more time, this would have been a shorter letter."

First, let's identify the root causes that undermine good communication. The opposites of brevity—waffling, droning, repetition, or other forms of boring an audience to death—occur because of predictable and avoidable issues that are best resolved before you tell a story. Surprisingly, editing too much, too soon to achieve the perfect "sound bite" or "elevator speech" can prune your story too soon and thus cripple its power to communicate.

Most of your storytelling occurs during personal conversations, presentations, and informal interactions—this is the time to practice brevity. Make your mistakes and attempt various styles of editing when it doesn't matter so much, so that you have the skills when it does matter. As you practice you will discover the particular bugs in your system that hamper brevity: waffling due to internal conflicts, droning because you enjoy the sound of your own voice, excessive control needs, or lack of preparation. Most of these issues threaten us all at one time or another.

Start with what you know—actually what you believe you

know—about "selling an idea." Our larger culture and your organizational culture have imposed formal and informal templates
that pop into play when you sit down to think about how to
sell an idea (i.e., tell a story). These mental templates sometimes
conflict. When two sets of expectations or methods compete you
can end up looping through increasingly meaningless choices.
Remember the agony of the dreaded "mission statement" meetings. Before Scott Adams of *Dilbert* fame gave us access to David
Youd's Automatic Mission Statement Generator,[1] we gathered
with high expectations only to end up choosing words selected
less on the promise of a bright future and more on the basis of
ending the damn meeting. In any culture where objective clarity
(what, how, when) reigns supreme, the exercise of answering subjective questions—like *Who are we* and *Why are we here*—feels
ambiguous. *Why* and *who* are inherently ambiguous—which is
why we need story and metaphor to approximate concepts like
passion, service, and faith. The word-smithing goes on forever
when a group seeks impossible levels of clarity.

Hidden assumptions about professional presentations and
what is or is not appropriate can screw you up. If the basis of your
mental template of "a good presentation" is a highly objective,
linear progression with all relative information presented in bullet
points, you can end up with seventy slides that communicate less
than a three-minute story does. Test yourself: If you were going
to give a one-hour presentation on your most important project
and its relevance to the organization's mission, what would it look
like? Notice your mental "to do" list. I'm guessing that choosing
a PowerPoint template and identifying your bullet points is one
of the first things on your list.

I know one large organization where most presentations easily
include an average of seventy PowerPoint slides, called a "deck."
They spend hours formatting data, adding animation, images,
and graphs. I doubt they realize the impact this presentation format has on their thinking process. These hours feel like hard

work and provide the illusion of improved communication. Performance anxiety fuels hours of formatting, sequencing, and display that would be better spent pacing the floor—particularly if your floor pacing gave you time to deeply consider why anyone should care about these numbers.

Brevity is better achieved by turning the computer off and asking yourself the basic questions: Who am I, Why am I here, and What is the highest possible outcome of my presentation? This may not feel like real work because it involves a LOT of staring into space, going for a walk, even heading to the gym—but this is the work that builds a cohesive message. Be prepared for these questions to reveal incongruities, paradox, and conflicting values. That's why you are taking the time to ask the questions—unaddressed incongruities, paradox, and conflicting values are the root cause of waffling, superficiality, and lack of cohesion.

For instance, imagine a human resources manager speaking to her company "town hall" meeting in a status report about customer service. This is a big topic with guaranteed paradox and incongruity. If customer service means "the customer is always right," and yet the same company also asserts, "People are our greatest asset," this is a paradox. This HR manager can support both messages equally well with graphs, charts, nice photos of customers and employees . . . but what is her story? Which one is it? If a mean customer treats an employee like dirt—what do you do? Do you protect your most valuable asset or tell the poor employee to suck it up because the customer is always right? In this rare scenario, it is impossible to achieve both. However, that "rare" scenario carries a disproportionate amount of emotional weight. It is, therefore, the perfect place to tell a story about what is ultimately most important.

Numbers keep your message superficial because they ignore paradox and competing values. If you want your message to really "pop," take a stand on which value you choose at the point of paradox. This resolves the reluctance to commit for fear of exploitation. You are then free to pursue BOTH values—which is what we really want—up to the rare point where the two actually conflict.

Graphs tidy up reality whereas stories reveal the mess. Avoiding messy reality keeps your message clear but shallow. Facing messy reality isn't as treacherous as you might imagine. Taking a stand (e.g., saying, "Employees first") achieves clarity, brevity, and the power of a clear, clean message. It requires that you both respect and trust your audience. And the minute you make that decision, it rearranges your presentation into a story that sticks, and it helps you edit your graphs and numbers down to the vital few. Core values always compete at some point. It takes courage to call, in advance, which value you choose when two values conflict. The failure to choose—the failure to imagine that the conflict will arise—is a root cause of superficial presentations and uninspiring leadership.

Having the courage to make a tough call—between customers and employees, quantity and quality, structure and freedom—relieves not only your anxiety but the anxiety of an unresolved story. Resolving the ambiguity of your listener's reality into a meaningful story wins followers . . . and enemies.

Brevity and the clarity of a meaningful story reveals your personal feelings about an issue. Contrary to the "business isn't personal" myth, you have to have feelings before you can stimulate feelings in others. Trust, faith, passion, empathy—these are all feelings. The purpose of telling a story is to make the impersonal personal. Personal feelings are there anyway, you may as well be honest.

What *Is* Your Story?

I recently visited an old friend in the hospital. He and his wife are wealthy from a fitness equipment business, which they sold when he contracted Parkinson's disease. He is confined to a wheelchair. His wife wants to pretend nothing is wrong. She wants to curb his spending on home care. She thinks he doesn't need a driver. She controls his access to new cell phones and is tired of him dropping them. I sat in the chair by his bedside, flooded with my own solutions to his problem. But they were *my* solutions. You will sit in this chair someday if you haven't already. Someone you love or someone who works for you is a victim of unfair treatment but you can't fix it for them, only they can resolve the problem.

What does this have to do with brevity? The ambivalence of wanting to appear sympathetic and wanting to give someone a kick in the butt (or the wheelchair in this case) can trap you in a looping conversation. These loops cycle endlessly. New ideas are met with a "yes, but" rejection, followed by sympathy, which elicits more examples of feeling trapped, which trigger new ideas for change, and you are back to "yes, but." It's an infinity loop that you can focus like a laser once you are willing to choose one value over another.

I was thinking, "You ought to have three phones at all times because you are going to drop ALL of them. You have Parkinson's, fer crissakes." But his depression frightened me and I was very careful to put my needs aside and choose a story that met his needs. I chose a kick in the seat over sympathy—but once I chose I was free to do both.

I told him this story:

> A law firm hired me to teach storytelling, and one of the young female lawyers told a story about her dad. He was a famous litigator. People said he "invented hardball litigation." But he wasn't such a great dad. One night she was talking on the phone, like any normal fifteen-year-old, and her father burst into the room. He grabbed the phone and slammed it down, berating her that he

had been trying to call for over thirty minutes. He yelled some more and then laid out a ten-minute maximum phone time and stormed out. We could see the hurt move across her face. Then she smiled and said, "Two weeks later the phone company pulled up to our house to install my own private line. I called them myself and paid out of my own babysitting money. Problem solved."

Can you feel the brevity this story brings to what could otherwise be a preachy litany of positive thinking or "you poor dear" sympathy? After I told that story I said, "If a fifteen-year-old girl can do it, so can you." And then I shut up. To talk more would have diluted the power of the story. I let him talk instead. The story did its work. After crying about his wife's inability to make the transition to their new life, he put his fist in the air and said, "I can even get a Blackberry!"

Brevity demands that you trust your own judgment about what is most important here, now, today. Trusting your judgment usually requires that you trust your audience too. These tough choices become clear as you face the dilemma of choosing the stories that best tell who you are and why you are here. Choosing the highest outcome for your presentation is a rigorous process. Once you have resolved conflicting values and hidden dilemmas, editing for brevity is easy.

Too Soon to Prune

Brevity is best sought after you are clear on the big issues. If you seek brevity from the beginning—looking for the "sound bite" or the "elevator speech" from the get-go—you tend to think "we don't have time for the Who I am, Why I'm here, What-is-the-highest-value bullsh**." After all, you are going to edit most of it out, aren't you? Sure, but like vegetables strained out of a good broth, the flavors remain.

Chapter 11 had you seeking mountains of sensory data, and this one asks deep meaningful questions . . . only to realize you never use most of it in your telling. This is not a contradiction in advice; it is about a distillation process where you travel a particular sequence that refines complex issues and broad appeal into a powerful story. The breadth and depth of your investment shines through your story with brightness, intensity, and essence like a 100-watt bulb compared to a 30-watt bulb. Each bulb is the same size, turned on for the same three minutes—but one is more intense and reaches farther than the other.

Great artists and writers invest hours of time and attention in search of an elegant expression or a single line that says it all. Picasso's original sketches possessed a remarkable realism that rivals photography. And yet his representations in later years edited out the realism and distilled an essence of meaning so intense that one painting can represent epic levels of human experience. His painting "Guernica" brought me to tears in the same way the movie *Schindler's List* did. Consider the investment of time necessary to communicate all the emotions of a war in one painting or one movie.

This is a good ratio for us to remember. Millions of dollars and hours beyond reason are invested to create one experience. The painting that looks easy or the story that seems simple is usually the product of many hours of investment. Sure, there are times when the perfect story pops into your head and you go with it. But most of the time the perfect story is the product of flesh and blood experiences reported after self-examination and considered intention.

I love when friends call me to say, "I used a story and it rocked." Greg Fuson, a conference director, told me about a remarkably brief story that shows the kind of deep connection forged when you take the time to ask yourself: Who am I? Why am I here? and What is the highest outcome?

> Greg walked onstage to introduce the first-ever meeting of The Vine, a conference for developers who want to build social community, not just physical structures. In his arms he held his baby daughter. "I had the privilege of becoming a father twice this year—first my daughter, Anna, born seven weeks ago; and again today at the birth of this conference we are experiencing together. Being a father leaves me awestruck at the sense of responsibility I feel toward Anna: one human being taking care of another. I think the essence of community, in its purest form, is as simple as that: each one of us taking responsibility for the care of others."

That's brevity at its best.

* * * * *

Take your longest story and ask yourself: What is the central message I want to communicate?

_____

_____

_____

_____

_____

_____

Tell the story again and see if it is shorter this time:

_____

_____

Note

1. www.dilbert.com/comics/dilbert/games/career/bin/ms.cgi.

CHAPTER 13

Brand, Organizational, and Political Stories

FINDING BIG STORIES that capture the essence of an organization, candidate, or brand is the Holy Grail for many newcomers to storytelling. They seek the kind of story that resonates and "travels" like a virus. A story that is simultaneously personal and collective. A story that sweeps attention and conclusions to a desired position. During the Bush administration, the story that "Freedom is on the march" was powerful, motivating, and funneled new data (even contradictory data) to fit this story. This story is a war metaphor that transforms news stories within one frame: either helping to win or lose freedom. Complex "on-the-other-hand" news analyses take longer than a sound bite, seem to slow the march of freedom, and thus translate to losing freedom. Any opposition to "winning freedom" seems to oppose freedom.

While this story was running high, slower more considered interpretations felt risky, even passive. Many citizens (myself included) think that this story framed interpretations that funded questionable actions and reduced scrutiny for several years. But regardless of your politics, the "Freedom is on the march" story worked its magic. But, who chose this story? How did they choose it? What competing stories were also considered? Understanding the group processes that influence story creation and selection can be just as important as understanding the characteristics and crafting of such a "Holy Grail" kind of story.

The quality of any story chosen to represent a group or agenda inevitably reflects the quality of the decision-making processes and thinking routines used by the group. If the group is disorganized and in conflict, the stories told are likely to be disorganized, conflicted, and weak. When a group is cohesive, deeply committed, open to risk, and disciplined in the face of adversity they have a much better chance of divining a story that pulls from the universal well of meaning.

Borrowing from the language of myth, these bigger stories are archetypal stories that trigger deep personal recognition because they highlight universal patterns of experience/response that draws attention, brings meaning, and creates a sense of belongingness—like kittens attract kids. Fear is a very strong universal pattern. Urban myths demonstrate the stickiness of fear stories. Love, hope, and faith stories seem to need more energy, imagery, even self-discipline to travel as far as fear stories.

However, building a taxonomy or formula for the "big story" only gives you the illusion that you understand "how to" find or create magic stories. And even if it was more than an illusion, your formula does not teach you how to create group consensus on your newfound "magical" story. Even if you can produce the perfect story, you still have to convince everyone else on the team that your story is "it." Understanding the highly predictable dynamics of group process helps you navigate waves of emotion that push, pull, and tumble story ideas. When you seek "Holy Grail" stories, your experience and talent facilitating group decisions can be just as important as your experience and talent as a storyteller. Great stories often lose cohesion and magic by the time they are approved.

Creativity = Deviance

When I was in advertising, our creative team often mourned "magic" stories that were picked clean of all magic by nervous product managers measuring and evaluating subjective metaphors with objective criteria. They often responded to a story by imagining worst-case scenarios of misinterpretation, weighing perceived risk against some best guess at perceived gain. Their rational approach (ratios of high risk to questionable gain) did not allow them enough room to embrace distinctive (i.e., deviant) images.

I remember our creative team pitched a radio ad to capitalize on Ford's sponsorship of the Australian Open in 1994 by using tennis court sounds in the background, as well as the trademark sound effect of Monica Seles's grunt as she hit the ball. Because Monica Seles had won the Australian Open in 1991, 1992, and 1993, and because Australians love their sport, we were confident radio listeners would easily recognize the reference. But the product manager had reservations. He became fixated on the potential for listeners to find the grunt . . . unpleasant in some way. The creative team narrowed their eyes and one leaned forward and asked, "Unpleasant, how exactly?" Lines were drawn and while civility and "the customer is always right" language prevailed, the "story" of performance with "grunt" died in that room without a funeral.

That story may or may not have had the magic we thought it did, but its death on the cutting room floor had less to do with the value of the story and more to do with the power struggles between the individuals making the decision.

Creative ideas initially appear deviant because . . . well, they are. Creativity is, in essence, deviation from the norm. To prompt new conclusions and thus new behaviors from an indifferent or hostile audience requires new data or a new frame for old data. Either way you must deviate from an old norm.

Another story—probably not technically true, but "true"

enough to travel the halls of frustrated marketing and advertising executives—also targets this kind of default to objective, risk-based decision making. The story takes us back to 1978, in a Coca-Cola board room. Apparently the marketing and advertising gurus were struggling over the final decision to name a new lemon/lime soda they planned to introduce the next year. The favorite name of the creative team was "Mello Yello." When the product manager (always portrayed as the idea-killer) finally articulated his reservations, he said, "Mello Yello just . . . sounds like the name of a street drug." To which the creative director nearly leapt across the table to ask, "What in the hell do you think Coke is?"

Stories like these reveal that decisions on subjective issues are distorted when objective criteria oversimplify the ambiguity of subjective issues. Objective thinkers seem to think that reducing ambiguity is the same as reducing risk. Not so.

Choosing Without Ratios

Choosing the right story to communicate an archetypal "truth" to the "masses" depends equally on your group's imagination *and* your group's skill in nonrational decision making. Groups in the unfamiliar territory of images, metaphor, and emotion often seek relief by oversimplifying these immeasurable qualities and converting them into some kind of quantifiable criteria that will offer them a basis from which to make a rational (i.e., ratio-based) decision. This default to numbers doesn't make for a better decision, it just allows for an easier decision.

Another escape route to minimize creative risk and avoid difficult conversations is to lean too heavily on the opinions of the most powerful people in the group. This dependence strategy works just fine if that person is a brilliant storyteller. Having a genius storyteller at your helm is an ideal situation. Genius storytelling leaders like Martin Luther King, Jr., Henry Ford, and Jack Welch deliver stories that move huge groups of people to actions that turn visions into reality. However, most of us nongeniuses are stuck in committees with other nongeniuses, struggling with paradox, competing values, and diversity that swell and shrink our sense of cohesion on all big decisions, including "What is our story?" These are the groups sorely tempted to default to measurable outcomes, rules, and formulas in order for their decisions to be more "rational."

In her most recent book, *On Becoming an Artist*,[1] Ellen Langer cites recent research into the "illusion of control" that ruthlessly deconstructs our favorite habits of seeking rules, principles, and cognitive frames that guarantee a winning formula for success (i.e., "Whoever tells the best story wins"). Particularly in business, routines that have shown a track record of accelerating decisions and bringing products and processes closer to perfection take us further away from the imperfection of human emotions and human experience. These processes literally depersonalize work relationships and personal commitment to subjective ideals like quality service, excellence, and dedication. The better we get at acting like automatons, the less meaningful our stories become.

There are no magic formulas. All of the really important issues in life are ambiguous and subjective. Your definition of success depends on your culture, age, socioeconomic status, personality, and the recent events of your life. I've seen many groups locked in mortal combat over a compensation plan or reward system, as if there were a "right" answer. Subjective issues have many "right" answers. To find a story that makes your target market feel important again depends upon where you and they are, who you and they are, when you and they are, why you seek to engage them, and why they might want to respond. Whether you chose the answers to these questions or they were chosen for you, to whom/where/when/why you tell a story creates the context upon which you can build meaning. Most work groups do not have good skills in negotiating subjective issues.

Statistics (and I *love* demographics, psychographics, and nifty cluster analyses) help us begin to answer some of these questions. However, once we begin to select and test story ideas in focus groups, test campaigns, or simply by running them up the flagpole, it is important to stay aware that everything from this point on is a result of subjective choices *based on the questions asked.* I don't mean to degrade the value of research, but it is important to resist the urge to treat research results like "facts." In this subjective milieu the single most important advice I can offer is to stay personally involved.

If objective decision making is a methodology for making impersonal decisions, then our methodology for subjective decisions must be to keep them personally relevant. Personal feelings and personal observations are suddenly as valid as numbers when choosing a collective story that evokes strong feelings.

The more personal feelings that go into finding or selecting your group's story, the more personal that story will feel to your group and to all who hear it. Passion is a tuning fork that vibrates the soul of anyone tuned in to the same key. Outcome-based reductive reasoning is thinking from the outside in. Powerful stories originate from inside-out reasoning that resonates. There aren't many rules other than "seek and ye shall find."

When the seeking is done collectively, your group's story evolves as a collective expression. This begins with individual stories. Don't rush or neglect individual stories in favor of finding the collective story. This rush omits a vital step that can result in a weak story, a "story by committee," or a superficial story without emotional depth.

Storytelling as a Self-Diagnostic Process

Storytelling as a function of self-expression requires some level of self-examination. In order to tell you a story that communicates who I am and why I am here, I must spend a little time asking myself those questions. This is usually done at a superficial level as quickly as possible: "We manufacture electronics that entertain people and earn a profit for our company." Snore. Diving deeper to find more personal meaning is the only way to evoke a more personally meaningful story. Self-examination is difficult enough at the individual level, but at the group level, egos get involved, old disagreements surface, and ideological differences can turn adults into kids fighting over the front seat.

The self-diagnostic process that finds meaningful stories scares the hell out of people who aren't sure they are living meaningful lives. Anxiety flares when outside-in thinking tools are set aside for inside-out thinking tools. Once they reflect, most people do find their lives are plenty meaningful (if a little out of balance). However, the process of self-examination tests your faith that your organization and your group are basically good people with good intentions. Groups that avoid deep examination seem to me to be anxious that honest self-examination might expose hypocrisy or emptiness. I've found that anxiety to be overstated in most cases.

The storytelling process is best begun by asking individual members of the group to tell a story that expresses who they are and why they are here, personally. It doesn't require a formal process, and it isn't always necessary to share these stories. However, sharing the stories can avoid a lot of nit-picking later, because all members of the group will have shared both the difficulty and the fullness of using one story to communicate such a big concept as "who we are" and "why we are here."

First attempts at group stories are often highly aspirational in that the story is more about who we wished we were, rather than who we are. Stories that aspire to more than we can back up risk sounding hypocritical. A minister friend of mine defined hypocrisy as "a fourteen-year-old boy standing in the balcony holding his girlfriend's hand and singing: 'All that thrills my soul is Jesus.'" When you look at it, hypocrisy is usually fueled by shame or some sense that "who you are" isn't good enough. From that point of view, hypocritical stories are a much bigger problem than at first appears.

True faith in your organization is based in honesty. The process of self-diagnosis through storytelling forces your group to keep your eyes wide open while finding stories that fuel (or douse) that faith. Embrace *all* of the stories—even the stories that represent less than ideal aspects of your organizations. The level of reality you embrace will ultimately shine in the authenticity of the stories you eventually choose to tell. More importantly, your ability to face reality will also improve your group's ability to fix subjective problems (hypocrisy, poor morale, cynicism) rather than cover them up with spin stories.

Solidarity

Stories that mobilize active engagement trigger personal recognition: that's me, this is about my life, this impacts people I love. Belongingness and solidarity are response and cause. Too often belongingness is sought by matchy-matchy strategies that— with images of race, adopted jargon, and other imagined hooks— try to tie you to a particular demographic and say, "This is you." The problem with this approach is that it is an "outside-in" rather than an "inside-out" approach. Find stories where we are the same and you find a mutual connection. Their "outsides" will always be different. But as human beings, our "insides" share common elements that can leap across superficial distinctions to connect a much deeper level—the level at which myth operates, or as Jung might call it, the collective unconscious.

To illustrate one such universal connection, here is a myth about Eris, the goddess of discord. Most people have at one time or another personally experienced this situation from at least one of the roles of this story when working with a group:

Invitations to an upcoming wedding omitted the goddess Eris. All of the gods and goddesses were rather outcome oriented and wanted to have a good time. Eris had ruined many parties. They decided to omit her name from the invitation list, but Eris showed up anyway. She threw a golden apple that was engraved, "For the Fairest," into the middle of the room. The cat fight that resulted among Hera, Athena, and Aphrodite completely ruined the wedding. It ultimately led to the Trojan War when Paris awarded the apple to Aphrodite after she promised him the love of "the fairest of all women," Helen of Troy.

All groups deal with dissent. They may try to escape dissent or invite dissent intentionally, but the goddess of discord visits all groups that have big decisions to make. Finding a "big story" will lead to some dissent about which stories are good. This dissent will come invited or uninvited. The advantage of inviting dissent intentionally is that your story will be more robust. Storytelling that tolerates group differences within collective meaning offers enough solidarity to tolerate differences outside the group as well.

As an example, you and I are not gods or goddesses (except on weekends, maybe). Yet we recognize this story as both personal and collective. We know all about Eris and her apple. At different times we lived this story. Sometimes we were the ones who uninvited "trouble." Sometimes we were the trouble. I can only speak for myself, but I must admit to having been involved in a catfight or two. I began using the word solidarity more often after I read the following quote by Eduardo Galeano:

I don't believe in charity. I believe in solidarity. Charity is vertical, so it's humiliating. It goes from the top to the bottom. Solidarity is horizontal. It respects the other and learns from the other. I have a lot to learn from other people.

When our stories are sought and found from the subjective statement that "I have a lot to learn from other people," they invite difference and are infused with the kind of solidarity that causes people to think, "This is important." Solidarity in action creates more stories of solidarity. Gathering stories teaches you how to get outside your own experiences and experience life as others might. To sit in someone else's chair, to walk a mile in their shoes, this is the kind of research that produces stories that makes listeners feel important again—feel as if they belong.

Note

1. Ellen J. Langer, *On Becoming an Artist: Reinventing Yourself Through Mindful Creativity* (New York: Ballantine Books, 2005).

CHAPTER 14

Point of View

PEOPLE MAY *SAY* they want objective facts . . . but dig deeper and the reason they want those facts is always personal. Most behavior can be defined in terms of personal needs (as well as many other equally valid perspectives). We need to belong, we need security, and we need to feel that we make a difference in the world. All these needs can only be seen by certain subjective points of view. They come into view and slip from view depending on the point in time and space from which you view. Every person you seek to influence can't help but evaluate your message from their subjective point of view. In order for your stories to be compelling to others, your stories must feel compelling from their point of view as well as your own.

A presentation skills class may have taught you to "read your audience"; this is similar but not the same. Using a story-based way of understanding your audience gives you more opportunity to feel what they feel and see what they see—from the inside out. The goal is to intentionally be less objective and more personal. Only a personal connection can generate the kind of empathy that causes them to reciprocate with empathy toward your position. This is just about impossible if you don't like or respect your audience. The primary stumbling block that sabotages most attempts to influence is a lack of respect for, or trust in, the people one is trying to influence.

People can tell when you don't respect them. The clues are tiny but impossible to hide. Political conversations are a good situation to observe how even the most polite words can fail to hide disrespectful opinions. Even family members, who love and respect each other deeply most of the time, can flip into an attitude of disrespect that destroys their opportunity to connect across divisive topics. The tone, facial expressions, and body language will always give away the story you are telling yourself about your audience. If a middle manager gives a report to senior management, secretly thinking they are a bunch of idiots and that his presentation will be futile, chances are his presentation will be futile. These nonverbal communications may never reach his or senior management's awareness, but negative feelings distort interpretations anyway. Most presentations of vital importance are between two groups that harbor secret stories that discount or discredit the other. Senior managers may think some workers join unions to exploit that power and compensate for failed careers. School teachers think the principal is really a pawn. The CEO thinks board members are already biased. There are a thousand stories out there that may leave you feeling "right" but that keep you from being connected.

Truly influential storytelling comes from the ability to step in and out of different points of view. This is another application of perceptual agility. Up until now we've practiced flipping back and forth between objective and subjective points of view. Now we go pro, by developing your ability to jump through time and space so you can "see" your story from multiple points of view. This skill will improve your storytelling in two ways. First you can find a point of view from which to respect just about any audience—they will hear it in your voice and it will smooth even the most ruffled fur. Second, you can re-view your most important stories from different character or time points of view. This process richly develops details and depth that pops your story from being one dimensional to three- even six-dimensional vibrancy, and it invites understanding from many different perspectives.

Is Bias Bad?

Bias isn't good or bad. Bias is unavoidable because your body can only be in one place at a time and you have lived in a certain time and place that created your perceptual frame. The fad of using objective thinking to "remove bias from decision making" may have led you to believe that unbiased decisions are possible. Objective decision-making tools encourage you to remove or ignore bias as if, once removed from the decision-making process, bias goes away. Bias doesn't disappear; it simply continues to frame interpretations without your input. Ignored bias, personal feelings, and emotional reactions can dramatically sabotage the success of "unbiased" decisions.

Since unbiased decisions can never be implemented in an unbiased environment, it's a good idea to investigate the sources of bias and familiarize yourself with relevant points of view and the biases they produce. In the same way that no person can experience life without bias, no story is without bias. A story without bias is boring because it becomes disembodied, sterilized, and dehumanized. Bias is a function of all behavior and thus of all stories that influence behavior. So own it, and demonstrate that you aren't blind to, or blinded by, your personal bias. Switch into several points of view and include details that provide evidence you know and understand several points of view.

By practicing shifting points of view, you will enrich your storytelling and your ability to "read a room." One fun example comes from Gregory Maguire, who decided to tell the story of the Wizard of Oz from the Bad Witch's point of view. He ended up with a new book, *Wicked: The Life and Times of the Wicked*

Witch of the West, and a successful Broadway musical. There is no telling what can happen when you develop this amazing skill.

Point of view alters meaning but, more important to you, point of view is also what *creates* meaning. Choosing a time, place, and point of view from which to tell a story is what makes a story feel like a real experience. Using your story to travel through time and space can demonstrate how many equally valid points of view you see. Remember the story in Chapter 1 about the farmer and his horse? Each day's experiences framed the horse he found as lucky or unlucky. There is nothing right or wrong with these shifting points of view. Since our bodies are subject to time and space, the only way to experience life is from a subjective point of view. The trick is to learn how to mentally and emotionally transport yourself into other points of view. By learning what others know, seeing what others see, and connecting to others, you earn the right to ask them to visit your point of view as well.

Here is a simple example:

1. *Objective Point of View:* Employee X's attendance is down 25 percent and performance levels indicate two missed deadlines.

2. *Employee X's Point of View:* A staff member tells you that Employee X recently lost his three-year-old child in a drowning accident in the family's backyard pool, and that he and his wife are getting a divorce.

3. *Staff's Point of View:* Most of your staff have been saving up their own vacation time to donate to Employee X to help him take more time off.

Objectively you might be justified in firing this person. However, from at least two subjective (humane) points of view you would risk your entire team's morale and might earn a new reputation as a heartless monster. Examining important decisions by using stories from several points of view can save you a lot of grief. You can avoid hurt feelings and time wasting resentments if you take the time to examine your most important stories from several points of view.

Exercise

Take one of your Vision stories and rewrite it twice from the point of view of two other characters.

First, pick a nonhero from your story and retell the story from the beginning to the end from that character's point of view. Sometimes this is fun and fascinating and sometimes it seems ridiculous. Do it anyway.

Next, write the story again from the point of view of someone who "loses" something in your original version of the story. For example, one of my Vision stories in Chapter 8 was about Galileo and how he managed to continue to tell his truth and avoid burning at the stake for it. This exercise meant I chose to research and reimagine Galileo's story from the Pope's point of view. The Pope was losing control over the church's dogma (and potentially, from his point of view, losing souls) every time Galileo spouted his heresies. As a result of rethinking this story, I began to see that like many leaders, the Pope may have agreed with Galileo but had an obligation to keep peace in his organization. The organization wasn't ready to incorporate this new truth without losing credibility. Seeing this point, I am able to use this story to facilitate understanding in fractious situations where bosses and heretics come to empathize with the good intentions of the other. This story can reach organizational leaders in a way that validates their power while at the same time it points to the possibility of peaceful collaboration. This is cool stuff.

Write your story from a "loser's" point of view. Choose any character who in your Vision story might end up feeling as if they lost status, power, autonomy, or something else of value. Ham it up and give yourself over to their point of view. This is a creative exercise, so have some fun with it.

_____

_____

_____

_____

_____

_____

_____

_____

_____

_____

_____

_____

_____

_____

_____

_____

   This exercise should have proven one of two possible alternatives: Either your Vision story can be told inspirationally from several points of view, or—and you need to know this—your Vision story is motivating only for you. "Hero" Vision stories often feed the ego of the teller more than the needs of the group. Using this exercise will save you from making a mistake. Having a strong ego is vital in taking a leadership role. Keeping that ego in check is equally vital to those who must decide whether they want to follow your leadership.

Use this exercise anytime one of your stories isn't working. You may discover that your story, or your telling of it, unintentionally disregards the point of view of someone vital to your success.

CHAPTER 15

Story Listening

IF YOU REALLY want to tell stories that win, first identify and listen to the stories and metaphors *already* winning minds and framing reality. Begin with the stories you tell yourself. It's amazing how unaware we can be of the stories that run our lives. Whether your story is that "life is like a box of chocolates" or "life is a bitch and then you die," you carry your beliefs around in the form of stories and metaphors. In order to meet people where they are—you need to know where you are. Examine the stories embedded in your mind and environment. You can't wallpaper a story of hope, trust, and integrity onto disillusioned, stressed out, and cynical stories—the new stories peel right off again like water-based paint on enamel.

Mapping the Mental Terrain

What are the stories that frame your perceptions? Stop and ask yourself: What is my story about hope? This is a very important archetypal story that, if mismatched between you and your audience, can sabotage your chances for success. Does your story paint hope as naïve? Or does your story about hope get you up in the morning? Before you make another presentation about a future project, I recommend you stop and listen to the stories that are operating right now in your mind and in your audience's minds.

This process feels awkward. To ask a coworker, out of the blue, "Tell me a story about hope," is a bit weird. It's easier if you lay some groundwork. Give them a reasonable basis for the question. For example, say, "I'm trying to get a fix on how we approach projects, and I need your help. This doesn't have to apply to your job, but what was your last experience with hope?" Be prepared to stay silent during any strange looks.

Steer them away from hypothetical or existential discussions. Keep asking for a concrete example: a story. If necessary tell your own story about a recent or important experience of hope. Don't force your story or theirs to move in the direction you would prefer. That will give you a false reading on reality. Don't worry about outcome yet—this is a process of mapping the mental terrain. You don't draw maps based on where you wish the mountains were. Useful maps show where the mountains actually are.

Seek first to understand the currents and riptides that govern perceptions. Only then can you dive in and reach your outcome. The discipline of mapping the mental terrain by listening to currently active stories arrests any urge to focus too tightly on desired outcomes. This space before you focus on the stories you want people to believe helps you see what stories they already believe. Understanding the current stories and allowing yourself to *be influenced by* these current stories will build the desires and expectations of audience into your story. The key is not only to hear the stories but to let them do their work on you. This may unravel carefully constructed plans—but better now than later.

Listening for Stories

Great storytellers are compulsive story listeners. Great artists seek out art. Great chefs like to eat other chefs' food. Writers read voraciously. If you love it, you seek it out. For those who love storytelling, listening is easy.

But what if you don't love it? Perhaps instead of listening to stories you would rather read a magazine, listen to music, or have bamboo shoots shoved under your fingernails. Hey, storytelling/story listening is not going to be everyone's favorite pastime.

The bare minimum level of story listening required to keep your skills fresh and stay in touch with your audience is an important decision to make. I can't give you a number of hours or percentage ratio, because it's not the quantity of listening as much as the quality of listening that counts. Describing the quality of listening required is tricky. Training courses in active listening are often classic misapplications of objective, measurable criteria when seeking a subjective, qualitative result. In the effort to break listening down to observable behaviors, "active listening" training may teach you about holding eye contact, nodding, leaning forward, paraphrasing back, and making reassuring noises (e.g., "um-humm").

I like to joke that these classes only teach us how to fake listening. One time when I made that joke a Hungarian woman in the back of the room raised her hand and said in a Zsa Zsa Gabor accent, "Yes! Listening is just like sex." I jumped right in, "How so?" She replied, "Ven ze desire is there, the skills will follow." She's got a point.

The desire to listen is also defined as curiosity—the same kind that killed the cat. Other desires take priority over listening. In fact, the reason most people don't listen is that they have other things they'd rather do. They are so focused on meeting ego needs, quelling anxiety, or moving into action, they literally can't listen.

I remember a chief of staff at a hospital challenged this idea. He said, "I ask people all the time to tell me what's going on and they sit there mute like bumps on a log." His impatient tone and the metaphor he used to describe staff—"bumps on a log"—

betrays the low quality of listening this otherwise well-intentioned man offered his staff. I imagine he engages in watch checking, facial gestures of incredulity, eye rolling, or other cues that teach his staff despite his questions he doesn't really want to hear anything but agreement.

The Opposite of Listening

Someone once told me, "Listening is the period of time I must wait until I get to speak again." At least he was being more honest with himself than Mr. Bump on a Log. A definition of listening—like all subjective issues—risks loosey goosey, imprecise language easily discredited by "rational" folks seeking clarity and focus. Hardliners threatened by the uncertainty of listening usually attack with sarcasm. Ridicule is an excellent way to avoid listening. We all do it at one time or another.

Whether your face correlates to your internal critique or you have mastered the poker face, the damage is done. Listening to internal "B.S. Alerts," "Whacko Alerts," or "Jerk Alerts" means you have stopped listening to the speaker and have begun to slice, dice, categorize, and judge the speaker's words, intentions, and meaning. This is a natural reaction when you listen to people you wish to influence. By definition, you are engaging someone with opinions different from your own. Therefore, the listening part of your influence process will require you to listen closely to stories that may contradict your own story. Holding your story at bay while you fully experience others' point of view without judgments is the key to real listening. Therefore the trick is to find out what you are doing that is the opposite of listening, and just stop doing it. Easier said than done.

Our world moves so fast you are pressured to make sense of incoming data as quickly as possible. Speed and focus have become unquestioned values applied to communication. People mindlessly try to improve communication by increasing efficiency (speed) and focus. That's great when you seek only to inform. However, when you seek to influence, speed and focus narrow the bandwidth across which you communicate. Narrow connections produce less influence. Listening is slow and wide rather than fast and narrow. Sort of like cleaning up a mess faster with a heap of paper towels applied in a slow, wide sweep rather than one (more efficient) towel quickly rubbed back and forth. Mindless speed and focus are the culprits of most bad communication. Rush or oversimplify conflicting elements and you may just miss the leverage point that would change their minds. If you rush past what people find hard to express you lose opportunities.

You might wonder, isn't listening all *about* focus? Aren't you focusing on the person telling the story? Well, yes and no. It depends on why you are focusing and how you focus. If your focus is wide and receptive—if you are willing for their words to change how you think—then yes, that's the kind of focus that draws true feelings and meaningful stories out of people. However, if you focus only on weaknesses and opportunities to distort, exploit, or contradict, then you could use a little help. The recent book *Presence: An Exploration of Profound Change in People, Organizations, and Society* by Peter Senge et al.[1] devotes about 300 pages to this idea, which could be summarized in two words: "Show up." For some people two words is enough, for others 600 pages would still not be enough.

True listening is a function of being present to other people's words and meaning even when, or especially when, their words and meaning might potentially disconfirm or destabilize your own. It's easy to listen to someone who thinks like you think. But you don't need help influencing people who think like you do. Listening to those who don't think as you do is what earns you the right to hear and retell powerful stories that build connections. When you understand another's story so well you can retell it with its meaning intact, your retelling affirms that you are who you say you are (a good person) and here for the right reasons. If you don't take the time to know your audience well enough to prove it by repeating back their story, they are likely to decide you don't have anything to say that they want to hear.

The kind of listening that earns you a turn telling your own story is the kind that requires you to stay connected to another person's point of view on seemingly irreconcilable differences, at the expense (temporarily) of your own point of view. This kind of focus feels more like surrender than "focus."

Is Listening Dangerous?

I read a quote somewhere that if anyone ever listened to the whole story of any one woman's experience in the world, the universe would crack in two. Listening to stories means staying present to collective human experiences with their wonder and atrocity. My friends who work with HIV/AIDs research, in social services, and in other types of community work have learned that good listening requires boundaries. If you do nothing but listen to sad stories, you might drown in sorrow and hopelessness. The line of people ready to tell you stories about bad things is much longer than the line of people waiting to tell you stories about good things. Sometimes I see people in the for-profit world, or even those who are action focused, treat listening—the real kind, where you let your guard down—as much too risky for forward progress. It is true that genuine listening can cede control and risk manipulation or exploitation.

Listening is not something you do all the time without end. It is a choice based on what you can process and how important it is for you to make a connection. It's not like handing the keys to your brain over to a stranger. You are still in charge. True, genuine listening *feels* risky, but you don't abdicate decision making just because you slow down and completely process another person's point of view. Listening may take you someplace you didn't think you wanted to go. Listening may reveal trouble about which you were blissfully ignorant. Still, listening always makes you smarter and gives you more connections to work through and with.

Good boundaries and a solid sense of who you are and why you are here gives you the stability and stamina to find the stories that reveal the core values and beliefs of those you wish to influence. You may have to surf over looping repetitions, blue sky perkiness, and a few angry tirades, but eventually the waves of meaning will appear as patterns both to you and possibly, for the first time, to them.

Ending at the Beginning

Whether you spend your time gathering stories or telling stories, the skills are reciprocal. If you think, "I don't have any stories to tell," you invalidate yourself and the people around you. Listen for stories. They are all around you. Go on a scavenger hunt for stories and you will find amazing stories. Finding stories is a personal one-on-one exchange. Forms and surveys are impersonal and predetermined by the questions they ask. Get out there and do some full body research. Don't send someone else to find your stories for you. Finding stories is its own reward.

Often people don't recognize how their life experiences are the basis for incredibly compelling stories. If it was meaningful to you, it can be meaningful to others. Do yourself a favor and go on an agenda-free hunt for stories about hope. Come up with your own first so you have one to offer in trade. Tell and hear the stories that create your organization's, country's, and family's future as hopeful or hopeless. Tell and hear the stories that define what it means to "win." These stories will teach you everything you need to know about influence and about storytelling.

* * * * *

Repeat as needed.

Note

1. Peter M. Senge et al., *Presence: An Exploration of Profound Change in People, Organizations, and Society* (New York: Doubleday/Currency, 2005).

Call to Action

EVERY PROBLEM IN THE WORLD can be addressed—solved, made bearable, even eliminated—with better storytelling. This book should give you tools to make more money, increase cooperation, and decrease resistance in any situation. It also gives you some tools to help you to make a difference in the world.

If your passion is to change the world for the better by ending poverty, protecting human rights, improving education, connecting "haves" with "have nots," or simply alleviating the paralyzing sense of isolation that comes with economic injustice . . . I'm your girl.

E-mail me or write, and I will help in any way I can.

Annette Simmons
Group Process Consulting
1006 Courtland Street
Greensboro, NC 27401
groupprocessconsulting.com
336-275-4404
336-275-4405 (fax)

Bibliography

Angelou, Maya. *I Know Why the Caged Bird Sings*. New York: Bantam, 1973.

———. *Singin' and Swingin' and Gettin' Merry Like Christmas*. New York: Bantam, 1997.

———. *A Song Flung Up to Heaven*. New York: Bantam, 2003.

Armstrong, Karen. *A Short History of Myth*. New York: Canongate, 2005.

Brodie, Richard. *Virus of the Mind: The New Science of the Meme*. Seattle, Wash.: Integral Press, 1996.

Cash, John R. and Patrick Carr. *Johnny Cash: the Autobiography*. New York: HarperCollins, 1997.

Cialdini, Robert. *Influence: Science and Practice*. Needham Heights, Mass.: Allyn & Bacon, 2001.

Cleveland, Harlan. *Nobody in Charge: Essays on the Future of Leadership*. San Francisco: Jossey-Bass, 2002.

Close, Henry T. *Metaphor in Psychotherapy: Clinical Applications of Stories and Allegories*. San Luis Obispo, Calif.: Impact Publishers, 1998.

Collins, Jim. *Good to Great: Why Some Companies Make the Leap . . . and Others Don't*. New York: HarperCollins, 2001.

Cooper, Robert K. and Ayman Sawaf. *Executive EQ: Emotional Intelligence in Leadership and Organizations.* New York: Grosset/Putnam, 1996.

Downs, Alan. *Secrets of an Executive Coach: Proven Methods for Helping Leaders Excel Under Pressure.* New York: AMACOM, 2002.

———. *The Half-Empty Heart: A Supportive Guide to Breaking Free from Chronic Discontent.* New York: St. Martins Press, 2004.

Gilbert, Daniel. *Stumbling on Happiness.* New York: Alfred Knopf, 2006.

Gladwell, Malcolm. *The Tipping Point: How Little Things Can Make a Big Difference.* Boston: Little, Brown, 2000.

———. *Blink: The Power of Thinking Without Thinking.* Boston: Little, Brown, 2005.

Glimcher, Paul W. *Decisions, Uncertainty, and the Brain: The Science of Neuroeconomics.* Cambridge, Mass.: MIT Press, 2004.

Godin, Seth. *All Marketers Are Liars: The Power of Telling Authentic Stories in a Low-Trust World.* London: Penguin Group, 2005.

———. *Permission Marketing: Turning Strangers into Friends and Friends into Customers.* New York: Simon & Schuster, 1999.

Goleman, Daniel. *Emotional Intelligence: Why It Can Matter More than IQ.* New York: Bantam Books, 1995.

Katherine, Anne. *Where to Draw the Line: How to Set Health Boundaries Every Day.* New York: Fireside, 2000.

Lakoff, George. *Don't Think of an Elephant: Know Your Values and Frame the Debate—The Essential Guide for Progressives.* White River Junction, Vt.: Chelsea Green Publishing Company, 2004.

Lamott, Annie. *Bird by Bird: Some Instructions on Writing and Life.* New York: Anchor Books/Doubleday, 1994.

Langer, Ellen J. *Mindfulness.* Reading, Mass.: Addison-Wesley, 1989.

———. *The Power of Mindful Learning.* Reading, Mass.: Addison-Wesley, 1997.

———. *On Becoming an Artist: Reinventing Yourself Through Mindful Creativity.* New York: Ballantine Books, 2005.

Lawrence-Lightfoot, Sara. *Respect.* Reading, Mass.: Perseus Books, 1999.

LeDoux, Joseph. *The Emotional Brain: The Mysterious Underpinning of Emotional Life.* New York: Touchstone, 1996.

Levitt, Steven and Stephen Dubner. *Freakonomics: A Rogue Economist Explores the Hidden Side of Everything.* New York: HarperCollins, 2005.

Lewis, C. S. *Surprised by Joy: The Shape of my Early Life.* London: Fontana, 1956, 1982.

Lipman, Doug. *The Storytelling Coach: How to Listen, Praise and Bring Out People's Best.* Little Rock, Ark.: August House, 1995.

———. *Improving Your Storytelling: Beyond the Basics for All Who Tell Stories in Work or Play.* Little Rock, Ark.: August House, 1999.

Ornstein, Robert. *The Right Mind: Making Sense of the Hemispheres.* San Diego: Harvest Books (Harcourt Brace), 1997.

Pert, Candace B. *Molecules of Emotion: Why You Feel The Way You Feel.* New York: Scribner, 1997.

Schank, Roger C. *Tell Me A Story: Narrative and Intelligence.* Evanston, Ill.: Northwestern University Press, 1998.

Schank, Roger and E. Langer, eds. *Beliefs, Reasoning, and Decision Making.* Mahwah, N.J.: Lawrence Erlbaum Associates, 1994.

Seligman, Martin. *What You Can Change and What You Can't: Learning to Accept Who You Are.* New York: Fawcett Columbine, 1993.

Senge, Peter M. et al. *Presence: An Exploration of Profound Change in People, Organizations, and Society.* New York: Doubleday/ Currency, 2005.

Simmons, Annette. *Territorial Games: Understanding and Ending Turf Wars.* New York: AMACOM, 1998.

———. *A Safe Place for Dangerous Truths: Using Dialogue to Overcome Fear and Distrust at Work.* New York: AMACOM, 1999.

———. *The Story Factor: Inspiration, Influence and Persuasion through the Art of Storytelling*, 2nd edition. Boston: Basic Books, 2006.

Suroweicki, James. *The Wisdom of Crowds.* New York: Doubleday, 2004.

Taylor, William C. "Get Out of That Rut and Into the Shower." *New York Times*, August 13, 2006.

Index

About the Author

One client described Annette Simmons as "willing to go into the jaws of the lion." In 1996, she founded Group Process Consulting to accommodate her diverse interests in research, writing, consulting, training, and facilitation. She has facilitated dialogue between conservative and gay Christians, budget-hungry military officers, and teachers and parents struggling to agree on educational methods. Her paying clients range from federal agencies like NASA, the IRS, the FDA, city and state government, to companies like IBM, Microsoft, and BestBuy, large professional associations, and small privately held firms.

She says she wrote her first book, *Territorial Games: Understanding and Ending Turf Wars at Work* (AMACOM, 1997) instead of getting a Ph.D. "It was a dissertation without the committee meetings." While consulting on turf wars, anonymous polls of work groups reported perceived levels of trust between group members from zero percent to 90 percent, with the average trust levels hovering just under 40 percent. This led her to write *A Safe Place for Dangerous Truth: Using Dialogue to Overcome Fear & Distrust* (AMACOM, 1999). Ten years of facilitating dialogue left Annette convinced that "sharing true stories is more time- and cost-effective in increasing trust than ice breakers, trust falls, ropes courses, or group hugs." Her last book, *The Story Factor: Inspiration, Influence, and Persuasion through the Art of Storytelling*

(Basic Books, 2002), was revised and published in a second edition in 2006. Her books have been published in Spanish, Portuguese, Chinese, Japanese, Korean, Taiwanese, Swedish, Norwegian, and German.

Annette has been featured on CNBC's "Power Lunch," radio stations including NPR, and quoted in *Fortune*, *Working Woman*, *The Chicago Tribune*, *The Washington Post*, and dozens of other newspapers and magazines. She wrote a chapter for *Best Practice: Ideas and Insights from the World's Foremost Business Thinkers*, published in 2003 by Bloomsbury. Annette currently resides in Greensboro, North Carolina, with her Italian greyhound Lucy and a squirrel with unauthorized access to her attic.